That Makes Me Mad!

John L Arnold

Published by Giles Corey Press, 2025.

Table of Contents

That Makes Me Mad!

Lessons in Psychotherapy

A Memoir

John L. Arnold

Copyright

THAT MAKES ME MAD! — Lessons in Psychotherapy - A Memoir

First edition. June 6, 2025.

Cover art concept by author with technical assistance from Bill "Magwa" Keener and James "Gus" Gilmore

Diagram "art" by author

Dedication

To my children, Jonah, Dylan, and Iris.

And my late wife, Lorel Meyers, the bravest woman I've ever known who taught me the lessons of meaningful relationships.

And to the hundreds of clients who took the risk of therapy and were instrumental in helping me learn more than I ever learned from books.

Acknowledgments

With gratitude to Ally Kornelis for her assistance in preparing the manuscript for publication and to Giles Corey Press for crushing it.

My fondest thanks to Tobias A. Ryan, PsyD who practices in Portland, Oregon/Vancouver, Washington for his technical support, professional review, and personally thoughtful commentary regarding the manuscript.

My deepest appreciation to Kristen A. Lindquist, PhD, professor of Psychology and Neuroscience at the University of North Carolina, Chapel Hill, (and soon to be associated with "The" Ohio State University) for her review of the book's premise. Dr. Lindquist's groundbreaking research and articles on the subject of emotion and language, and their relation to culture, are highly recommended for more exacting scientific background.

Special thanks to first readers Christine Arnold, Sabine Pacher, Elizabeth Arnold, and Bill "Magwa" Keener, for their interest, suggestions, and commentary.

Love and appreciation to my son, Dylan Meyers in China for being intrigued with languages, and for his insights regarding Chapter 2... along with the technical help and advice rendered to his tech-impaired dad in dealing with the digital world as is required with a manuscript to be published.

Similarly, to my friend and author, Marco Etheridge, in Vienna, Austria for his support and sharing of his writing experiences, and to his lovely wife, Sabine, for her feedback, and taking time to read this manuscript.

To the Village Idiots motorcycle club whose friendships and appreciation of recreational mischief reminded me to take important tasks seriously without taking myself too seriously.

To my therapist, "Gert", without whose wisdom this book would not have been possible.

My heartfelt thanks to my friend and colleague, Ray Burleigh, for his courage and support inside the social service bureaucracy that tries hard but often falls short in not shooting itself in the foot.

My undying appreciation goes to my clinical mentor, the late Allen Ewig, whose professionalism, integrity, and leadership was instrumental in laying the foundation for my clinical career. His knowledge included the wisdom to know when to "sit on his hands" and let his staff figure out their own lessons.

My thanks and gratitude to Lynn D Johnson, PhD who was the mentor that never knew me.

In memoriam to my late friend G. Russell Carpenter, former United States Air Force nuclear missile launch officer and one of the finest, and unknown, epistemologists of the 20th century.

In memoriam also to my late friend and teacher, Gordon L. Shadwick, who challenged and mentored me into adulthood.

And in loving gratitude to my wife, Christie (Cox) Arnold, whose understanding, indefatigable support, and unconditional love provides the blessings I try daily to deserve.

Preface

Apart from presenting some additional psychotherapeutic practice ideas that were helpful to me and my clients, this book is about a cultural discrepancy between what most people believe about how emotional feelings are generated and how we actually act in our daily lives. In brief, most reasonable people believe they are responsible for their emotions and behavior — taking responsibility for one's feelings and actions is generally accepted as a pro-social no-brainer. Yet, on a daily basis most of us unwittingly attribute our feelings, and sometimes our behavior, to someone or something other than ourselves. To wit, in our common vernacular we hear ubiquitous refrains like "That makes me mad.", "He pisses me off.", or "She drives me crazy." These types of commonly heard phrases inherently infer that the creation of our feelings is caused by other people or events. The premise of my suggestion is that these comments are not simply a figure of speech or an irrelevant issue of semantics. Indeed, they are embedded not only in our language but in our cultural psyche and subsequent behavior as a result of this largely unexamined discrepancy. More importantly, I'm suggesting that this discrepancy facilitates not only a lessened understanding of the mechanisms of emotional control but is an obstacle to our attempts at self-actualization, increasing self-esteem, and promoting contentment.

This proposition can be somewhat provocative. Although I haven't yet presented anything that is likely to provoke dissonance, when someone says "Actually, other people don't make you feel, you make yourself feel" it can conjure up confusion and pushback. (Don't ask me how I know.)

If four therapists are together for clinical group supervision and I ask, "Who's in control of and responsible for your feelings?" the usual answer is "Well, each one of us, of course". However, if I follow that question up with "So why do you think it is that likely before the day is up you might blame other people and circumstances and even inanimate objects for how you feel?", the group will look a little confused and might eventually even start arguing or imagining that I'm simply playing some kind of intellectual word game. The idea that other people and things "make us feel" is as irrational as the psychotic symptom of "thought insertion" where the person struggling with a psychotic illness has a belief that some other person is responsible for their thoughts. In daily practice we live in a culture that has the arguably collective psychotic belief of "feelings insertion". But because this language is endemic to the culture, it cannot be considered a psychotic delusion.

Despite the number of times a kid who is asked why they hit someone replies "S/he made me mad!", grownups are not likely to accept the hitting as a reasonable response any more than a judge accepts this defense in a courtroom. Yet this childlike reply is common. Nonetheless, adult variations of this response are equally common in situations where we irritate ourselves.

The purpose of this book is to share what I hope is information that can be helpful to others, especially those that are ambushed by anger and irritability, which includes laypeople and clinicians alike.

What's weird about the basis of my premise is that I didn't make it up. It's not new. It's all been said before. It's already been written in literature from great thinkers, spiritual leaders, social and neuro scientists, none of which I am. If there's anything profound about it, it's that the discrepancy doesn't seem to be specifically examined.

For instance, in recent years much has been written about anger and yet much of that discussion continues to use the phraseology that suggests the locus of control of emotions resides outside of ourselves and, hence, seemingly outside of our control. The fact is that each of us is the regulator of our emotions. Initially something untoward or unexpected happens and we react. The nature and degree of our reaction comes from within us, not without. But even writers that *do* recognize that the mechanisms of emotional control come from within, and can be altered, will use language inconsistent with their recognition. For example, in his wonderfully insightful and useful book, *Anger*, the great Buddhist teacher Thich Nhat Hanh writes "When someone says or does *something that makes us angry* [emphasis added], we suffer." I suggest that part of the reason for this, again, has to do with what's embedded in the popular parlance, and what isn't. It's the same reason that "I-messages" (See chapter 5) are challenging to master. Plus, we're certainly not practiced at saying things like "I irritated myself with that." And even if we do, it sounds funny, and others think you're strange. It's as if we have no common language for taking responsibility for our feelings.

I should note that these ideas have not resulted in my own immunity from the evolutionary holdovers of the primitive parts of our brains that facilitated the survival of Homo Sapiens (to be explained later in this book). But I will say that my amygdala (that part of the brain that has in part to do with emotional control) has, since my childhood, been significantly "tamed". (See Catherine Pittman, Ph.D.) I now am happier and have less health-impairing angst coursing through my body. As Lynn Johnson, Ph.D. wrote "this is an achievable goal." The examination of this discrepancy also represents concepts that I believe can be a faster, simpler path to goals for clinicians and their clients as well as people generally.

I am encouraged, too, by discovering that my hope for the utility of the implications regarding the book's premise and the Anger-Loss model (See Chapter 4) herein is supported by recent research describing a broader, more "constructionist" view of emotion creation (See Kristen A Lindquist and/or Lisa Feldman Barrett). In her widely acclaimed book *How Emotions Are Made*, Barrett says of emotions "They are not triggered; you create them."

———————

I once had this thought that psychiatrists shouldn't title their own books. Although I'm not a psychiatrist I'm guessing the same might apply to me... but the title is my doing anyway.

I also had a theory about how good therapists came to write books. It went like this: A therapist does therapy and is pretty effective. Friends and others said, "You should write a book." Presumably in an effort to be helpful to others, the therapist did. But effective therapy doesn't actually have much to do with technique, even though it is often the primary explication in the book. But according to research, only about 15% of what is effective in therapy has to do with technique despite the fact that the bulk of a therapist's time and money for learning how to be more effective is spent on learning "techniques". (See Scott Miller, Ph.D., et. al., *The Psychotherapy Networker,* "No More Bells or Whistles")

What tends to get left out of the effective therapist's book is the unique Self and personality that was actually key to making any technique work. Yet these personal characteristics are rather difficult to self-describe. And I won't pretend to describe mine.

Regardless, my desire to write this book has to do with my confusion about why the previously described discrepancy doesn't seem to be specifically articulated in the literature of mental health practice. Of course, therapists are a part of the culture, not apart from it. For example, we were hardly in the forefront of the women's liberation movement. We were actually then more likely to come up with diagnoses of hysteria for women who were traumatized in abusive relationships.

Be that as it may, my hope and purpose for this book is as stated above despite that I don't pretend to be a scholar or academic. I haven't even thought that I had the self-discipline or skills to write a book. And I'm certainly not doing it for fame and fortune. In fact, whether or not this even gets published, I will be satisfied if I simply get a manuscript done, for myself, before I shed the mortal coil.

———————-

When I was in graduate Social Work school at Portland State University and learning about different theories of personality development, psychological paradigms, and the multitude of techniques that arose from them, I wondered when my coursework would cover some kind of synthesis of these — some metatheory or the "One Ring to rule them all". My ignorance and naïveté waned eventually but nonetheless I realized that there was some unspoken suggestion that as a would-be therapist, I was expected to choose among these, and which was going to be the foundation of my own practice.

Much later, after the slow realization that my own unique Self was the primary tool around which my practice would evolve, I stopped looking for the Mother of All Therapies.

After I had been given the responsibility and privilege of being a clinical supervisor, I found myself being asked by a form that I had to fill out for a state licensing board on behalf of a supervisee: "What theory base or therapy does the supervisee use in their practice?" Uh-oh. In addition to the use of *their* own unique Self, I realized the person I was supervising likely was using whatever I was using, but I didn't know what that was in words because I had never been required to articulate it. So, I wrote "*Strength-based*"[1] *approach within a bio-psychosocial perspective. Theory base borrows from CBT and social learning models.*

Techniques are evidence based and influenced by problem-solving/ solution-focused, skill building, and trauma-informed approaches." That sounded good enough to me, and passed muster with the licensing board, but despite trying to be honest and accurate, it was a listing devoid of practice wisdom.

"Practice wisdom"? During my first several years at a psychiatric day treatment facility for children I read that, on average, the most substantive work that a client initially achieved in therapy occurred during the first 8 to 10 sessions. As the agency's family therapist, that statistic seemed to ring true with my experience. With the thought of trying to maximize those first sessions I had the idea that if I attended a Brief Therapy workshop, I might be able to more quickly be effective. I happened to attend a workshop with Lynn Johnson, Ph.D., a noted Brief Therapy and Positive Psychology practitioner out of Salt Lake City. It was a seminal move on my part. I not only learned that brief therapy didn't have to do with brevity but was informed that the business of doing therapy took a lot of practice. Lynn suggested that it took about 8 to 10 years before you might feel like you were "turning a corner" and actually might be on the threshold of knowing something useful. Coincidentally, including and prior to graduate school, I had been doing work for about 10 years and was just beginning to feel a little less like a fraud when I was with my clients.

If I could make people feel, I'd make them feel happy. I hope you find this little book useful.

—John L. Arnold, 2025

Chapter 1
A Bag of Wind

"There is nothing either good or bad, but thinking makes it so."

—Hamlet, Act II, Scene ii

Years before I started a private practice I was given the opportunity to be the clinical director of a psychiatric day treatment center for children and families, the workplace I mentioned in the preface. I loved the job and the staff with whom I worked. Despite being located in a relative backwater on the Oregon Coast, we also had a consultant who was one of the best child psychiatrists in the state. Having had a good deal of experience pre-graduate school with residential treatment and milieu therapy in the Bay Area of California where I was fortunate to have a very special director who became my clinical mentor, I felt at home.

However, despite being blessed with a wonderful spouse, great young children, and an old farmhouse on an idyllic 20 acres in the country, I wasn't feeling at home when I was at home. I was prone to irritability and anger. I didn't realize how bad it was until I "lost my temper" with my wife. I was shocked by my behavior.

The incident prompted me to get back into therapy, my second time in 10 years, and with the same therapist. This time it was because of Anger.

My therapist was a near 80 year old woman that in spite of our difference in practice techniques, I trusted.

I told her what had happened with my wife and that I needed some anger management — the go-to phrase and format for anger control.

Calmly, and without judgment, she matter of factly said "anger is a bag of wind".

What?! Like thin air that blows? I come to therapy for anger management and my goal was being discounted? Was she not going to tell me how to manage my anger? Fortunately, I trusted her and intuitively knew there was, again in my life, something new for me to learn.

Of course, learning is different than *applying* what you've learned. She was the first (and so far, the only) person who told me that other people didn't make me feel. She said ***I*** made myself feel, that I was the one in which the emotions I felt were created. I had trouble getting my mind around that. What?! You mean there's nothing I can do but accept the nonsense of others and just put up with it, not assert myself in the face of things I objected to, things I didn't think were right? No, of course not, but that was a different lesson, one I wasn't yet ready to deal with.

With respect to my wife, our relationship became the primary context within which I practiced and began to un-learn a lifetime of socially and culturally reinforced programming. My therapist (whom I'll refer to here as "Gert") said weird things like my task was to find my wife's "center of love" and, in effect, pay attention to her intention, not my interpretations of her behavior. That's the trouble with intention: you can't see it, you can only see behavior that is in turn subject to your interpretation.

So, there I was, stuck with the discomfort of unfamiliar ground. I spent months practicing the letting go of those negative reactions to my spouse's behaviors. I spent months accepting that her behavior belonged to her and not to play the fool's game of trying to change that over which I had no control. I spent months trying to focus exclusively on changing me. I even began to get practiced using my irritated and angry reactions as a signal to look within myself for what it was about me and my expectations that was triggering my emotional response. It wasn't easy.

But I loved my wife. And I knew she loved me. I accepted, at least intellectually, that her intentions were never designed to cause me hurt but rather to change things for the better, regardless of my interpretations of her behavior. Besides, my goal was to change me, not her. If she wanted to change something in herself, that was her business, not mine. I had enough of a challenge trying to deal with myself.

I realized I must be making some kind of progress when she and I were outside one day doing some work when she said, "Will you call Gert and make an appointment for me to see her?"[2] Obviously she'd been thinking about her own need to do some personal work. She had seen a local therapist before (Gert was located out of town) but for whatever the reason she wanted to try Gert. I have no idea if changes she may have perceived in my own behavior during the past several months had anything to do with her request. My reply to her request was uncharacteristic of any that I'd ever made to her. I found myself saying "No. That's your business to do." In response, my wife screamed "Fuck you!" and stormed into the house. My emotional reaction to her was also uncharacteristic, something I had never before experienced. I felt an inner calmness in the face of getting yelled at by the person I loved. I somehow knew that what I'd said was the right thing for myself, let alone her. Subsequently, she made an appointment on her own.

————

Empty Boat. *A monk decides to meditate alone. Away from his monastery, he takes a boat and goes to the middle of the lake, closes his eyes and begins to meditate. After a few hours of unperturbed silence, he suddenly feels the blow of another boat hitting his. With his eyes still closed, he feels his anger rising and, when he opens his eyes, he is ready to* *shout at the boatman who dared to disturb his meditation. But when he opened his eyes, he saw that it was an empty boat, adrift, floating in the middle of the lake... At that moment, the monk achieves self-realization and understands that anger is within him; it simply needs to hit an external object to provoke. After that, whenever he meets someone who irritates or provokes his anger, he remembers; the other person is just an empty boat. Anger is inside me.*

—Thich Nhat Hanh

———-

I had a high school client who I'd been seeing for awhile. I don't recall what we were talking about — something about interactions with others. Suddenly he looked at me and, as much to himself as to me he said "It's always about me, isn't it?

"You are the universe experiencing itself."

–Alan Watts

Chapter 2
Language & Thinking?

"A different language is a different vision of life."

—Federico Fellini

I am not a linguist and, to my detriment, speak only English. Nonetheless, it occurred to me that doing some cursory researching about how language might influence thinking and perception would be a good idea given the premise of this book. The manner in which the popular expressions of how emotional causation is attributed to external events is so commonplace in American English (if not elsewhere) that it seems to provoke cognitive dissonance when first introduced despite the evidence for the premise being corroborated by neuroscience. Initially, it certainly provoked conflict in me and, in my experience, it often does so in others.

Because my personal and professional experiences have benefited so much by examination of this discrepancy between our language and neuroscientific knowledge of how emotions are regulated, I thought it might be useful to create some "dissonance within the dissonance" by looking for evidence that language plays a role in what seems to be a general reluctance in the acceptance of this book's premise.

As previously stated, it is not uncommon for people to think the argument is a spurious one, one that has to do with merely an overthinking of a semantic artifact or a silly intellectual word game.

When I was an undergraduate at U.C. Berkeley I read a book by Edward T. Hall titled *The Hidden Dimension.* Hall was an anthropologist who explored and researched cross-cultural relations. It was the first time I was introduced to the idea that one's culture, including its language, was a sort of bubble inside of which can define and limit how we come to know things. Epistemology is the study of knowledge, the theories of "how we come to know." Before reading his book, I had never considered that there were different ways of knowing. Once I understood that, I realized that I "knew" and began to "understand" in different ways.

I had a friend who obtained a Ph.D. in some strange field like the "theory of knowledge and ethics of philosophy". He was driving cross-country, from Vanderbilt University where he taught, to the west coast. He was waxing on to a friend traveling with him about some social event with which he was concerned and passionate. In fact when he told me the story it was clear that he had been ranting. I forget what the subject was but his friend was getting himself so flustered with the stridency of my friend's diatribe that he finally grabbed my friend and said "Russ! Not everybody *thinks* like you!"

There are different ways of thinking, different ways of knowing things. Many years ago I found myself listening to a morning radio show of Paul Harvey's, one of my Dad's favorites. Harvey always ended his show with a story (along with a chipper "Good day!"). That morning it was a story about the solar eclipse that was going to take place later in the day. According to my recollection, he said in Arizona today there was going to be a solar eclipse. A group of Hopi Indians would point their bows at the jaguar that was taking bites out of the sun and would shoot the jaguar with arrows in order to kill or scare it off so that the sun could return. "It will work", he said. According to scientific thinking, there's no relationship between how the full, life giving brightness of the sun returns after an eclipse and this Hopi ritual. But for the early Hopis, this way of knowing is perfectly sound. It works. It is of related interest that the Aztecs had a similar ritual regarding solar eclipses and jaguars. Hopi and Aztec Indians are considered distantly related by ancestral ties, geographical proximity, and because both belong to the

Uto-Aztecan language family, meaning they share a common linguistic ancestry. The Hopi people are believed to be descended from the Ancestral Puebloan people, who are also linked to the Aztecs.

Regardless, it wasn't surprising for me to discover that the relationship between language and thought has been a subject of discussion for many years, and not just in modern times where knowledge has been influenced by a "scientific" epistemology and the language derived from it. Charlemagne, the ruler of the Frankish Kingdom in the late 700s to early 800s in the common era (CE) is quoted as having said "To have another language is to possess a second soul."

It turns out that how language can affect perception has been an area of research for many years. Lera Boroditsky, a cognitive scientist, wrote an article in the *Scientific American* titled "How Language Shapes Thought". In 2011 she writes "Research in my lab and in many others has been uncovering how language shapes even the most fundamental dimensions of human experience: space, time, causality and relationships to others." The article begins with a story taking place in Pormpuraaw, an Aboriginal community in Australia where the researcher asks a 5 year old girl to point north. Without hesitation she does, pointing precisely north as confirmed by compass reading. When the same question is asked of scientists from prestigious universities at a conference, they point to all different cardinal points and everything in between. They haven't a clue. This phenomenon is then related to language differences.

There's evidence indicating that people who speak languages relying on absolute directions are surprisingly good at keeping track of where they are, including in unfamiliar landscapes or inside unfamiliar buildings. They are better at this than people who live in similar places but do not speak such languages. This suggests that the requirements organized by their languages "train" this cognitive ability. (See the work of psycholinguists Stephen C. Levinson, Max Planck, and John B. Haviland.)

I once read in a Michael Crichton novel, *The Rising Sun*, that in the United States we have a tendency toward asking the question "*Who's* to blame?" or responsible for some event while in Japan there's more of a tendency to ask, "*What's* to blame?" Until recently, I didn't know if there really exists some general cultural difference about this but you can watch most any U.S. news broadcast about a significant disaster or mishap and will find that questions of "who's responsible?" are much more likely to be asked than questions that explore the more complicated and useful circumstances of "what's responsible?" While doing some research for this book I discovered that there's some truth to this cultural difference. The evidence is related to cultural language differences.

In the same article referenced above, Boroditsky wrote about their study where English, Spanish and Japanese speakers watched videos of two guys popping balloons, breaking eggs and spilling drinks, either intentionally or accidentally. She said "Later we gave them a surprise memory test. For each event they had witnessed, they had to say which guy did it, just like in a police line-up. Another group of English, Spanish and Japanese speakers described the same events. When we looked at the memory data, we found exactly the differences in eyewitness memory predicted by patterns in language. Speakers of all three languages described intentional events agentively [actions of a particular person or thing], saying things such as 'He popped the balloon', and all three groups remembered who did these intentional actions equally well. When it came to accidents, however, interesting differences emerged. Spanish and Japanese speakers were less likely to describe the accidents agentively than were English speakers, and they correspondingly remembered who did it less well than English speakers did. This was not because they had poorer memory overall — they remembered the agents of intentional events (for which their languages would naturally mention the agent) just as well as English speakers did." She also wrote "English speakers tend to phrase things in terms of people doing things, preferring transitive constructions like 'John broke the vase' even for accidents. Speakers of Japanese or Spanish, in contrast, are less likely to mention the agent when describing an accidental event." In that case the Japanese and Spanish speakers were more likely to say "the vase broke". Apart from the implications this might have for witness testimony in a court of law, the difference in connotation could facilitate an exploration of how something came to be and what might be done to correct things in the future rather than a single minded focus on establishing blame.

In the early 1900s Edward Sapir and Benjamin Whorf introduced the idea that one's language influences thinking. What's come to be known as the "strong" version of the so-called Sapir-Whorf hypothesis (a.k.a. "linguistic determinism"), which claims language limits and determines human knowledge or thought, has been largely discredited. But the debate regarding the "weaker" version of their theory referred to as "linguistic relativity" versus the "linguistic universality" suggested by Noam Chomsky and others can give a linguistic ignoramus like myself a migraine. Getting tangled in the weeds of this debate is well beyond the scope of this book.

Nonetheless, apart from the complexities and stridency of the debate, there are some very general conclusions that might be gleaned regarding how language can influence thought. For instance, leaning toward the universality side of the argument, psychologists Eric Lenneberg and Roger Brown who did some studying of the Alaskan Inuit's different words for "snow" versus English speakers single word, conclude both groups are able to discriminate between different types of snow. Meanwhile psychologist Alfred Korzybski's therapy program of "General Semantics" in the 1920s leaned toward the linguistic determinism side of the debate but Korzybski's method was seen as one that produced effective results.

Boroditsky simply concludes "...The structures of languages can make it easier or harder for us to learn new things."

I have a good friend in Austria, an English-speaking American who is an author and writes prolifically. His wife, a native Austrian who speaks English as a second language, is his primary proofreader. She offered her talents to proofread this manuscript. I told my friend it was amazing to me that someone speaking English as a second language could be a good proofreader for English writing. He said that was the very reason she was so good at it. He said "she sees through different eyes".

The pushback I've mentioned regarding this book's premise is common. I only recall one time where a client immediately seemed to understand the concept of the problem I've described about the discrepancy between our language and what neurology tells us about the expression of feelings. He was a doctor in a medical practice. His accepting response was tantamount to a forehead slap when he said "Oh, that makes so much sense!" But we're all on our own path. His just happened to be a short one before moving on to whatever his next life lessons were.

A more common and relatable phenomenon is how different experiences can alter our perception. I was involved with community theater, primarily as an actor. But occasionally I participated in different production roles. I was once the managing director of a play. A theater friend said, "you will see this play with different eyes – eyes that no one else has." He was right. It's not unlike reading a book written by someone you know – or seeing a friend or family member on stage in a play for the first time. It is initially a weird experience, a new experience. New experiences result in new perceptions, new perspectives. It's not much of a stretch to understand how a change in the use of our language can also lend itself to a change in perception.

One of the concepts that practicing clinicians are familiar with is that of "reframing" – the rephrasing of something negative that describes instead a positive aspect of the issue. This is one of the most commonly understood examples of how a change in language can facilitate a change in thinking, a change in perception. An example might be when a client is describing symptoms of depression. Just the discussion of that subject itself during a therapy session can create a depressive atmosphere or context. But if the therapist were to make a reference to how sensitive the client is to the negativity in the world, the context of "depression" can begin to change to that of a personal virtue, i.e., one of emotional sensitivity or a capacity for empathy. If the therapist also introduces this "reframe" with enthusiasm, which demonstrates the opposite feeling state of depression, the entire context of the presenting problem can begin to appear more positive, a "problem" that is simultaneously a strength. This change in perception can facilitate a more positive foundation for the challenging work of defeating depression. (See the *Journal of the Association of Psychological Science*, "The Psychology of Framing: How Everyday Language Shapes the Way We Think, Feel, and Act" by Stephen J Flusberg, Kevin J Holmes, Paul H Thibodeau, Robin L Nabi, and Teenie Matloc)

Nonetheless, embracing the idea that others don't "make us feel" emotions is a significant challenge. For instance, regarding the interweaving of culture, language, and emotion, consider Aretha Franklin's 1967 iconic rendition of the Carole King-Gerry Goffin song "(You Make Me Feel Like) A Natural Woman". The song is certainly embedded in the Millennial's brain. Younger generations who may not be that familiar with Aretha likely are familiar with the song. If sung by a woman, the connotations of gender subjugation get a cultural "pass". And generally nobody, except the author, would have thoughts that she's actually the one that's making herself feel. But, of course, changing the lyrics would understandably be seen as bad poetry. The song is woven into the cultural fabric, as is the notion that other people are in control of our feelings.

Regardless of the science, it's clear that changes in our thinking, through changes in our language, can be helpful to our process of becoming. If we can *know* in a different way, we can think differently about the language that may help keep us from understanding how we can better control emotions that organize us into regretted and self-sabotaging behaviors.[3]

"Change your language and you change your thoughts."

—Karl Albrecht

Chapter 3
The Brain
"HomeoSapien" Equilibrium[4]

"Between stimulus and response, there is a space. In that space is our power to choose." —Viktor Frankl

I'm going to present a grossly oversimplified version of the neurological mechanisms of brain function that are pertinent to the discrepancy that this book is examining — the discrepancy previously described between how we each generate emotional responses and how we mistakenly credit other people and events for "making us feel." For the oversimplification, I apologize in advance to the neuroscientists everywhere who have made significant contributions to connecting and corroborating neurological processes with psychotherapy. (See Louis Cozolino, Ph.D, *The Psychotherapy Networker*, "It's a Jungle in There")

Regarding the "oversimplification", the drawing of the brain in Diagram 1 is actually obsolete with respect to more recent advances in neuroscience because it grossly under-represents the complexity of neural interaction among brain structures and networks as well as the interrelationship with the body as a whole. Even use of the term "Limbic System" is now considered out-of-date. Although I was a bit chagrined when reproducing here the drawing of the brain I used for years in my practice (See Diagram 1), I giggled at the memory of my occasionally bringing my ceramic Phrenology head by L. N. Fowler to clinical supervision groups. I used it as a reminder that what we see as the truth of neuroscience today likely won't be the truth tomorrow. In the early decades of the 19th century Phrenology, the evaluation of personality traits and other mental attributes by determining the topography and size of bumps on the skull, was influential in psychiatry and psychology. (See "**The Bed of Procrustes**" and importance of cautious judgment in Chapter 7.)

The "body as a whole" includes the brain and is functionally integrated despite the human tendency to examine holistic systems in discrete parts so we can better understand each. This segmentation, of course, tends to be done at the expense of understanding the nature of the interrelations of the whole. In her groundbreaking synthesis of the recent advances in neuroscience as it relates to the holistic creation of human emotions, Lisa Feldman Barrett writes of emotion "They are not universal, but vary from culture to culture. They are not triggered; you create them. They emerge as a combination of the physical properties of your body, a flexible brain that wires itself to whatever environment it develops in, and your culture and upbringing, which provide that environment." Nonetheless, this "constructed" view of emotions is very much in keeping with the purpose of this book despite what the advances in neuroscience would say about the now antiquated depiction of the brain that was used as a visual aid in my practice. New or old, the Anger-Loss model described in Chapter 4 holds its utility. If emotions are constructed, they can be "de-constructed". Although neuroscience is still in its infancy, one wonders how we will know when it reaches childhood let alone its adolescence.

In my private practice I always had a whiteboard on the wall next to me so as to scribble words and images as visual aids for clients. I had this idea that, with the exception of those that are sight-impaired, most of us are "visual". Bandler and Grinder (See Neurolinguistic Programming (NP), e.g., *Frogs into Princes*) suggested that different people have different "representational systems" in how they process the world, i.e., some of us being predominantly visual, auditory, kinesthetic (feeling), olfactory (smell), or gustatory (taste). Over the years, the science of NP has been regarded as questionable. Regardless, I found that visual aids during a discussion were helpful to most all of my clients. (That and enthusiasm helped, too.)

So, during sessions I would draw very rough and clunky diagrams on my whiteboard with different colors to represent brain structures and exaggerations of neural pathways to represent brain connections. (See Diagram 1)

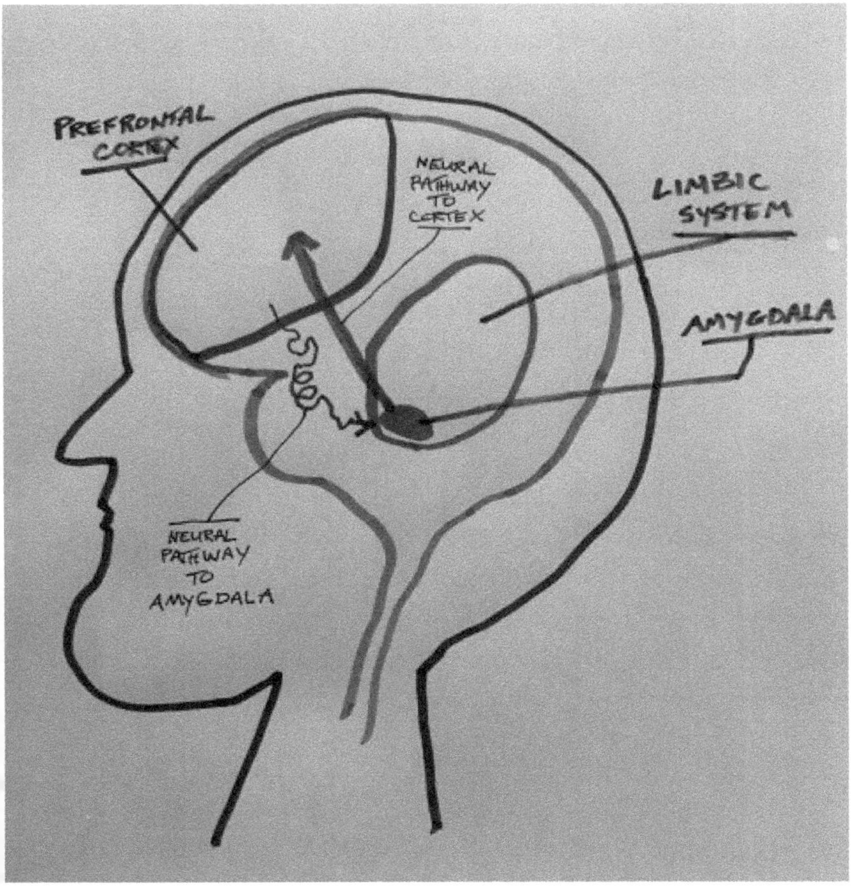

Diagram 1

Regarding the brain, I would draw a silly-looking human head, with a brain inside which highlighted the prefrontal cortex and the limbic system and which included the brain's amygdala.

The amygdala is a small, almond-shaped structure that is involved in processing emotions, especially fear, and social stimuli. The amygdala is largely responsible for our survival defense mechanisms of fight, flight, or freeze. It helps perform primitive but important functions. It helps answer primal but necessary survival questions like "Can I eat it?", "Will it eat me?", "Can I mate with it?", or, "Should I run like hell... or freeze in place in hope that it will ignore me?"

In order for these functions to be effective, the time between stimulus and response has to be very fast, like milliseconds. But consider the prefrontal cortex—the part of the brain that controls our complex cognitive functions. These include reasoning, decision making, the expression of personality, social appropriateness, executive functions like thinking and problem solving, working memory, and error monitoring in order to switch strategies when it's determined that an "incorrect" response isn't working.

These prefrontal cortex functions can take more time than is effective for survival. This isn't such a good thing if you're out in a grassland hunting for supper and a Sabertooth tiger jumps up from a gully. Your prefrontal cortex, with all of its wonderful complexity, isn't real helpful here — it's not a good time for contemplation. "Gosh, that's a Sabertooth with saliva dripping from its fangs. I wonder what should I do?"

To compensate for this, a comparatively robust and well-traveled neural pathway from the amygdala to the prefrontal cortex temporarily impedes the prefrontal functions. Yay! But in the process, you necessarily lose I.Q. points. Boo! Research suggests when your amygdala is activated your prefrontal cortex drops about 10 to 15 I.Q.

points. A workshop presenter once claimed it could be as much as 30 points. Either way, speaking for myself, I can't spare any.

Any strong emotion like fear, anxiety, anger, excitement, or joy can trip the amygdala switch and impair the prefrontal cortex. For example, if you were to substitute "stress" or "anxiety" for anger in this book, it would work equally well. In keeping with this book's title, I'll focus on the emotion of anger. If you ask the studio audience if they've ever done anything stupid when they were angry, most all but those that have personalities consistent with sociopathic narcissism will raise their hands.

Fortunately, there is a less traveled, less robust (and I always draw it as thin and circuitous) neural pathway back to the amygdala. This is the road to, dare I say our "better selves"? It is the road to getting that pesky amygdala to "switch" back and calm down. The good news (for the early survival of Homo Sapiens) and the bad news (for modern life) is that this brain-housed paradox of neurological functioning, albeit still useful, can be more easily solved than might be imagined. In fact, "imagining" might be seen as instrumental to the paradoxical solution.

Imagining is a cognitive function that requires thinking. Even though amygdala activation impairs the cognitive function of the prefrontal cortex, our higher functions are not necessarily inaccessible. It's just that they are impaired temporarily — and they are impaired before we "know" it. Knowing is thinking. This result in the evolutionary process makes sense in that survival is more important than thinking (as the confrontation with the Sabertooth reminds us). The importance of thinking is irrelevant if we're dead.

The problem is that we're not as likely to be confronted with life and death situations as we were, say, 150,000 years ago. And yet our brains still work similarly despite the more recent evolution of our neocortex. The primitive fear circuitry doesn't do a good job these days differentiating between real and imagined danger. We have the capacity to experience the anxiety of Sabertooth confrontation with everything from ephemeral financial concerns to being on stage in front of an audience to annihilation by an asteroid. Or, in keeping with this book's purpose, getting ourselves angry with everything from someone doing harm to a loved one to "not getting your way" to a minor, unmet expectation.

Back when I was first grappling with the new and seemingly crazy idea that my therapist introduced me to, the idea that it was me that made myself mad, along with its corollary that I could create feelings that were healthier and more useful, I had an unexpected experience. One of my least favorite things to do at my rural home was to go underneath the part of the house that was 75+ years old and into the pad and post constructed crawl space. On a Friday night I was looking forward to working outside in the garden with my wife and kids. On Saturday I woke up to a beautiful sunny summer day. When I walked by the house on the way to the garden, I was assaulted with the smell of sewage. Uh-oh. I peeked through the access hole and saw a large pile of raw sewage and toilet paper. (The sewage line from the toilet had broken and its deposits were on the floor of the crawl space.) I was pissed. In frustrated anger I donned my yellow rain slicker suit and reluctantly squeezed through the hole with a 5 gallon bucket and shovel. The more foul my dread, the more foul my mood. After the task began, I started thinking, about Gert, and somehow recognized the situation as one that could apply to this idea of creating different feelings. Yeah, right. Nonetheless, I tried to just get into the moment of it all, to not perseverate about the task, but to just do the doo. Unexpectedly my mood started to improve and the absurdity of it all gave way to humor. I started singing and making up verses to a poop song. My family who had previously been giving me wide berth were giggling out in the garden and asking questions about a new kind of craziness coming from the guy under the house. It was a great day. As the great songwriter, Greg Brown, asked in the title of a song, "Who woulda thunk it?"

So... in a simple way, thinking, especially when triggered by the emotions one is feeling after amygdala activation, sends signals back down that less well-worn path to the amygdala and begins to calm it down. For instance, if you anger yourself about something, and you were to then imagine that image in Diagram 1, you'd be starting to *think* instead of emoting. You'd be beginning to re-activate your temporarily impaired prefrontal cortex and begin to calm down. In the same way, if your toddler comes up to you distraught and crying over some real or perceived mishap and you could distract them with a hug or a kiss to their owie, or actually get them to "take deep breaths", you would in effect be helping them to *think* instead of their continuing to be emotionally awash with their recent mishap.

More than this, the more often that neural pathway is used, the more it becomes usable, more robust, and more straightforward so that it can carry more signals. Much has been written in the last 10-15 years about neuroplasticity, the regenerative properties of neurons and/or the ability of the brain to develop new or more effective connections.

Practice makes perfect. In his wonderfully intriguing, accessible, and enjoyable book, *The Talent Code*, the writer (not a neuroscientist), Daniel Coyle, does a remarkable job explaining how skills are achieved, including the effect of skill-building at the anatomical level in the brain. He essentially reminds us that practice makes perfect, but not just any kind of practice, rather something he refers to as "deep practice." It turns out that genetically endowed talent is largely a myth. Talents and skills are developed by specific practice. (See the works of K. Anders Ericsson.)

Scott Miller Ph.D., et. al., in their 2007 article, "Supershrinks" (*The Psychotherapy Networker*), describe a similar type of practice termed "deliberate practice". Deliberate practice requires (1) knowing where you're starting from and what exactly it is that you want to improve. (2) Being open to and actively seeking feedback about your progress. And (3) actively, and single-mindedly, practicing those specific skills that you're targeting. One of the nice things about this type of practice is that when you're nine for nine at the free-throw line and your 10th shot clangs off the rim keeping you from your goal of 10 for 10, you don't have to waste time, energy, and angst because doing so is not in keeping with the exclusive focus on simply getting better. You've merely fallen short of a psychic investment in an artificial, and unnecessary, expectation.

If we could look close-up at the neural circuitry that would be required for playing a guitar, or shooting free-throws, and then compare it with a close-up of the same circuitry after proficiency was developed, we would observe a very different, more complex pattern of larger gauge wiring. We get better at what we practice, including skills that quiet the amygdala. (Unfortunately, we also get better at everything we practice, including addictive behaviors, anger, and even depression.)

Simply thinking or distracting ourselves when emotionally triggered can facilitate quieting the brain and making the neural connection between the prefrontal cortex more efficient and effective. Conscious, slow breathing, for even 10 minutes while focusing on the experience of how the inhaling and exhaling feels is one of the easiest, most effective ways to do this. Breathing is core to relaxation and meditation techniques.

I mentioned "meditation" once to a client who asked, "Is that the thing where you close your eyes and focus on a purple ball?" Well, yeah, it could be. This particular client frustrated himself in his attempts at meditating. For him (like a lot of us), he didn't think he could do it. However, as with doing many things that are new, recognizing that we've gotten distracted from the process and then getting back to it helps rewire your brain such that it becomes easier and easier to stay on track. Practice.

Meditation, used regularly, not only helps calm and relax us but also gives us a working memory as to what a calm mind and body feels like. This, in turn, gives us a more experiential understanding of the goal we're trying to achieve. One writer defined meditation as "the daily practice of nonjudgmental awareness". That doesn't mean you don't hear what's going on around you, rather, you just passively acknowledge that it's there and let it be. Meditation is no longer seen as some woo-woo eastern, mystic religious practice. Its benefits have been corroborated by western culture and modern science. Proper breathing is the foundation of meditation. (See Lynn Johnson's "Autogenic Training").

How you breathe matters. Not only does breathing s-l-o-w-l-y help, but breathing "diaphragmatically" facilitates relaxation. The workings of the diaphragm have always been too complicated for me and my client's understanding so I prefer the term "belly breathing" (as opposed to chest breathing or a mix between the two.) During a challenging time in my life I very unexpectedly, and uncharacteristically, got involved in a community theater group. My involvement evolved into doing a lot of stage acting. As a part of warm-ups before performance, someone would always lead the ensemble in exercises. Inevitably this would include a breathing exercise where the leader would direct the group to breathe "diaphragmatically". Everyone in the group would begin taking "cleansing" breaths, whatever those were... and despite half the group having a confused look on their face.

Breathing exclusively with the upper chest, like at those times of high anxiety, can actually *increase* our anxiety. On the other hand, breathing exclusively with the belly, like an infant, decreases anxiety and facilitates relaxation. This is partly because we have to do it consciously (thinking), but also because it activates a trigger to the cranial vagus nerve which has a sensor located behind the belly and gets activated when the stomach is distended. If you're confused how to belly breathe, put your hands over your head (sitting, standing, or lying down) and you will belly breathe automatically. If you are sitting in a chair in public and want to relax without looking too weird, put your hands behind your back or the back of the chair, and you will belly breathe automatically. Of course, you can belly breathe without your arms extended by simply concentrating (thinking). When you *think* about it, it's easy.

For the time-conscious, it should be noted there is recent evidence that three controlled short term (5 minutes daily) breathwork exercises can improve mood and reduce anxiety as well as reducing physiological arousal more effectively than an equivalent period of mindfulness meditation. (See Andrew D Huberman, et. al., School of Medicine, Stanford University in 2023 Cell Reports Medicine, "Brief Structured Respiration Practices Enhance Mood and Reduce Physiological Arousal")

Regular exercise and physical activity also help to distract and quiet an overactive brain. Hobbies and other activities of interest are beneficial, too. Even mental health therapy can help. :^) All of these "techniques" and tools can help expand the metaphorical "space" between stimulus and response that was mentioned in the Victor Frankl quote at the beginning of this chapter.

About that space, I once had an experience when I was 20 years old and living in San Francisco. Although I embarrass myself now writing about it publicly, it was an unexpected and significant experience regarding that space between stimulus and response. I had gotten myself into a very angry state over some life event that I don't recall. I lost I.Q. points.

I picked up a ceramic coffee cup and cocked my arm back to throw it at the thick, solid wall of my apartment. In that very brief moment I was cognizant of asking myself "Are you really going to throw it?" I had never experienced a moment like that before, or since — a moment where my prefrontal cortex asked a question prior to a potential rage response. But the answer was "Yes!" and the cup hurtled to the wall and shattered. After calming, the pieces had to be swept up and the wall patched and painted. But the event was painted and framed in my brain for the rest of my life.

It's been said that there are no mistakes, only lessons to learn. At the time I didn't know what that lesson was but somehow knew it was a significant one for me. It wasn't just a cracked cup but a "crack" in the system of my previous experiences.

"Ring the bells that still can ring.

Forget your perfect offering.

There is a crack, a crack in everything.

That's how the light gets in.

That's how the light gets in."

—Leonard Cohen, *Anthem*

Chapter 4

The Anger-Loss Model

Paying Attention to What's Behind the Curtain

"Instead of looking under the dish and all over the table for what you want, don't forget to look on the plate in front of you." —Anonymous

John Bowlby's classic trilogy on attachment, separation and loss, gave us insights into the effects of loss. In Volume 3 he described one of his students processing grief from the loss of a loved one and the stages of denial, anger, despair, and partial acceptance that the student experienced. That kind of devastating loss is primal. On the psychologist's hit parade of psychological stressors, loss of child is #1 followed by loss of significant other.

However, I'm suggesting that "loss" is even more primal than that, though not as devastating as losing a loved one. "Separation and loss" is experienced throughout life, from the process of birth until the time of dying and death. Change is the essence of life, yet all change equates to a separation and loss before something new can begin. Fall to winter, winter to spring. And also including the much more mundane changes of hair growth and hair cutting, or traffic lights changing from green to red.

A lot has been written as to what it is that underlies anger, e.g., insecurity, confusion, or the need for control. One writer suggested that frustration could be behind anger. (I will suggest later that frustration is actually a type of anger.) I once suggested to a client that he sounded angry. He replied "No, I'm not angry, just frustrated."

Regardless, in the name of parsimony as well as accuracy, I suggest that *loss* underlies *all* anger, as well as the underlying change that has taken place. But first, let's think about the various forms of anger. I think of a lot of things as being on a continuum or a spectrum. In this case, anger, everything from little tiny anger to big anger. When talking to clients I would draw a continuum of anger on my whiteboard. (I would also acknowledge to the client that this is not a linear scale but just a subjective one.)

annoyance - irritation – frustration - anger - rage

(Yes, I included "anger" in the continuum even though I'm discussing the others as a subset of anger.) I was describing this to a middle school client who asked, "What about 'fury'?" When I got done laughing, I told him this was a great question and that from now on "fury" would be at the far end of the scale. I had another client, an older adult male, who I knew was angry but never manifested any obvious signs of those on the continuum. It took me weeks to figure out that his inherent impatience was a form of anger. From then on, "impatience" marked the beginning of my whiteboard's scale.

impatience - annoyance - irritation - frustration - anger - rage - fury

Expectations are the root of all evil. (That said, it should be noted that expectations are normal and useful, and we couldn't do without them. They help us plan. But the insidious, unrealized, and unrealistic ones are a bane.) The idea that loss initiates all of these deserves some explanation. The most common type of anger we feel on a daily basis is the littler feelings of anger, e.g., feelings like impatience, annoyance, and irritation. Underlying these are expectations that the world will work in certain ways that are favorable to us. Ha! Good luck with that. We are often unaware that we even have such expectations.

When I got to the public parking lot of my small office in a small shopping mall, I tended to park in the same place. Creature of habit. When that spot wasn't available, I became aware that I was very slightly irked. But because I had sensitized myself over the years to paying attention to *any* feelings on the anger spectrum, I automatically asked myself "What's that about?" As always, the answer was an expectation, in this case an unrealized one that "my" space would be available to me. Pretty silly to have the thought that it was *my* parking space. So, I giggled at myself for having that expectation and, over time, no longer irked myself with that event. I hadn't simply reduced the degree of amygdala activation so that I could better "manage" my tiny anger, I'd gotten rid of the feeling of being irked. The "loss" in this case was the loss of the parking space not being consistent with my unrealistic and unrealized expectation. If a client was late for an appointment, I might initially have a feeling of impatience. If time went by, and s/he was a no-show, I might find myself feeling annoyed. *If* I stuck with those feelings, especially if it was becoming a pattern with the client, I might not only reinforce and escalate my annoyance to feelings further down the scale, but more importantly I could lose sight of a therapeutic issue, namely, what were the client's goals and were those goals pertinent to the question "What else might the client be a no-show for in his/her life?" This kind of thinking freed up my mind to not operate with less I.Q. points but to keep a wiser focus on the goals my client had previously stated for themself as well as assisting me to stay focused on my professional role and obligation. Addressing a chronic habit of "lateness", or not showing up for obligations, could then be brought up but in a context that had to do with my client's issues, not mine.

The loss here, of course, was the unrealized expectation that my client would show up on time. More important to the purpose of this chapter, I'm suggesting that unmet expectations underlie all anger, including the bigger types of anger that reside further down the continuum.

If, contrary to your expectations, your spouse yells at you despite your best intentions, a neighbor shoots your dog, or you get a "C" on what you thought was a great paper you wrote, you'll likely experience higher levels of anger and be kept from understanding the situation in a manner that you can deal with more rationally. Thinking is rational, emotions, by definition, are irrational. The greater the psychic investment in an expectation, the greater is the likelihood of a bigger anger response.

Emotions are Irrational? A close friend was recently reading a draft of this manuscript and asked about the statement above regarding emotions being defined as irrational. She asked "Is this really a definition? ...I had no idea about that. I feel then that I am probably often irrational." *Rational* is defined as "being of or related to reason or logic". It is a cognitive process having to do with thinking that is related to the prefrontal cortex. Conversely, emotions are "instinctive or intuitive feeling as distinguished from reasoning or knowledge." This isn't to say that it is "irrational" to have emotions because we humans do, thankfully, have a capacity for emotions, for "feelings". Therefore, emotional responses are "logical" to have but they are instinctive and are not necessarily regulated by reason or "rationality". Therefore, they are not a rational process but instead are "irrational". Therein lies the evolutionary, paradoxical problem for human beings that is housed under the same roof that is our skull, as explained in Chapter 3.

Being irrational, i.e., emotional, is "normal" but it can get us into trouble in relationships because it may lead us into "unreasonable" behaviors. It may also help lead us into creativity, art, and poetry but that is a different subject than the focus of this book.

It's not surprising that there is confusion in our language between thoughts and feelings as exemplified by my friend's statement above when she says "I *feel* [emphasis added] then that I am probably often irrational." What she means, of course, is that she *thinks* she is often irrational. We commonly hear the word "feel" used synonymously for "think".

Fundamental Loss? Perhaps the most common, probably fundamental, loss that friends, family members, spouses and partners experience is the feeling of the *loss of connection* to one another. The drive for connection to others appears to be primal for humans. At the risk of overstatement, separation from those connections can be experienced as an existential threat. Hence, the anger, acted out or not, that may accompany seemingly minor squabbles with those we care about is understandable. When coupled with the real or hoped for safety of "unconditional love" in those relationships, it is no wonder that there's truth to the old adage that "you always hurt the ones you love".

Anger as a secondary emotion. (See Diagram 2 – a "whiteboard" drawing) The implication of what I learned from my therapist, "Gert", was that anger was a "secondary emotion". If you meander the internet, you'll find many references and descriptions of primary and secondary emotions. My version is as follows. Gert told me "emotions come from the head, feelings come from the heart." Usually "emotions" and "feelings" are words used and defined as being synonymous. I don't dispute this but have found Gert's head-heart distinction useful.

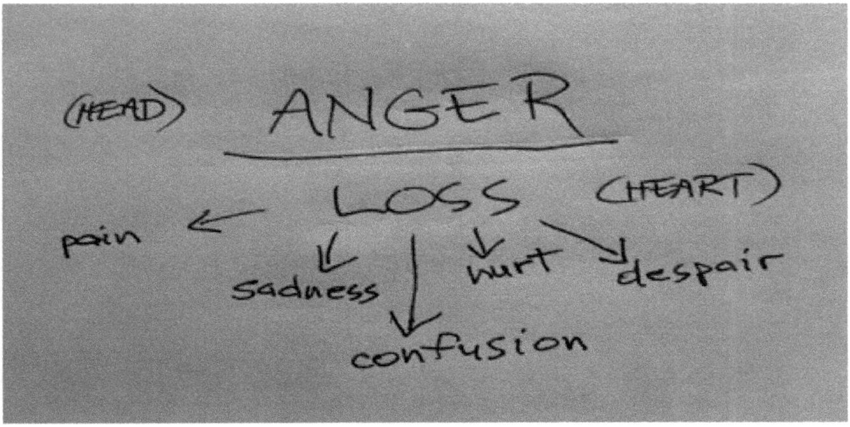

Diagram 2

Probably the first feeling we have when the amygdala is tripped is that of confusion. It usually doesn't last long, maybe milliseconds. Humans don't like feeling confused. We prefer having a feeling of mastery, and congruence with our expectations. Confusion triggers us to "make sense" out of disparate experience (like an unmet expectation). For instance, if we're driving on the freeway and a car unexpectedly cuts us off, we are not likely to remember that *we're* the one that chose to buy a vehicle and drive on a public road where stuff inevitably happens. Nor are we likely to wonder whether the driver of that car is dealing with an emergency. So, we quickly attempt to escape confusion by going to our head where we can quickly analyze and judge the moment at hand. Unfortunately, this usually involves blaming someone or something outside of ourselves for the feelings we've created. We're much more likely to shake a fist, or a single finger, at the "idiot" that cut us off and put us and maybe our family in danger. (I will say that driving on public roads is one of the more common circumstances in life that continues to provide me with lessons to learn.) My dad once jokingly said "First, we have to establish blame." I don't think he knew how often that was, indeed, the first thing we do.

Regardless, when we stay with our confusion, or use our anger as a flag or signal that there is something more important to deal with, we are in a better position to delay behaviors organized by anger. We are then practicing the thinking that can bolster the neural networks which can increasingly tame the amygdala – we are better able to use our optimized intelligence to more easily deal with others' behaviors and other events.

The idea that external events cause humans to feel. Reinforced by the popular perception represented in our language, we tend to subconsciously believe that external events cause specified emotional reactions. We say that a particular event or situation is "stressful" or that it makes us angry. However when, let's say, five different people experience the same event, it's easy to imagine that there could be five different reactions. More interesting is that those same five people could have, at different times, five reactions that are different than their previous reactions to the same event. Obviously, the difference doesn't have to do with the event but rather it has to do with the person, with their "mood" at the time of the event. In other words it has to do with something within the person, not something from the outside.

For example, within a close circle of friends, we may be accustomed to joking around with the use of sarcasm. We can usually say something to each other in a sarcastic manner that we all find humorous. But if someone happens to be in a negative mood at the time of the sarcastic remark, the targeted person might not find it so funny. Gert once told me "sarcasm is not humor". After thinking about it, I realized that context mattered. And the context was the other person's internal mood.

Thoughts underlie emotions, emotions underlie behaviors. People usually come to therapy because of troublesome emotions and/or behaviors. If we can examine the thoughts that underlie these emotions and/or behaviors, we are in a better position to change emotions and behavior. Much of this thinking is developed in early childhood and "registered" in our undeveloped childhood brains but we continue to hold on to these thoughts into adulthood. (See Erik Erickson's eight stages of psychosocial development.) Simply stated, we can change these underlying thoughts and reactions with our now more developed brains. We don't even necessarily have to know what these thoughts are in order to change them. We can even just imagine what those thoughts might be that underlie the troublesome emotions and behaviors. It is not uncommon for a client to engage in therapy with the idea that *understanding* what's going on will spontaneously change emotions and behaviors. (See *Understanding* Therapy (Part 1) in the Appendix) While understanding might be important to the change process, it's usually not enough. If we want things to change, we usually have to actively change something.

If we logically imagine what the thinking is that a troubling emotion or behavior might be linked to, we can examine as to whether or not it makes any sense. If, for instance, it bugs you that you always say "I'm sorry" to someone who has expressed a negative reaction, even when it has nothing to do with you, you might say "What's that all about?" You might imagine that it could have something to do with a parent's tendency to blame you for stuff when you were a kid even though there was no fault or intention on your part. You then might talk to yourself about becoming more sensitive to this automatic, apologetic reply and, in the future, your apologies would feel better and have more impact. When, in the old TV series *Happy Days*, Fonzi actually could get the words "I'm sorry" out of his mouth, it had quite an effect on who he was apologizing to. Or, in the case of less troubling emotions, like getting yourself "irked" when someone "steals" *your* unreserved parking space in a public lot, there's not much to understand other than your being stoopid and you can go straight to a new way of thinking that can rid yourself of feeling irritated. Giggling at yourself is healthier than feeling irritated.

ANTs - Automatic Negative Thoughts. (See ANTs in the Appendix) ANTs are a concept developed by Aaron Beck who introduced Cognitive Behavioral Therapy (CBT). Daniel Amen, a psychiatrist and brain disorder specialist is credited with coining the term "ANTs". ANTs is a simple format for examining negative thoughts that impede emotional development or organize us into unhealthy or unnecessary behaviors. The format has us ask ourselves four useful questions about these automatic negative thoughts — thoughts that can be about ourselves or others:

1. Is the thought true?
2. Can I absolutely know that it's true?
3. How do I act when I believe that thought?
4. Who would I be without the thought? Or how would I feel if I didn't have the thought?

Regardless, the primary ("heart") feelings (Diagram 2) that come from the loss of an expected outcome, unrealized or otherwise, subjectively feel worse than the secondary emotion of anger ("head" judgment). The feelings of confusion, hurt, sadness, and disconnection feel weak and wimpy. They're painful. Humans are wired to seek pleasure and avoid pain. Anger, while pretty useless, feels big and powerful. If we have to choose between feeling big and powerful (anger) vs. weak, wimpy, and hurt — the primary feelings of loss — our likely choice is pretty obvious. Someone once said "Angry is sad's bodyguard."

Nonetheless, when we go with anger, and get stuck there, we are kept from the primary feelings that could help us focus on the primary issues we all have that are necessary for resolution and increasing self esteem and contentment. While righteously ranting and complaining about the unfairness in the world, nothing is accomplished other than the dubious benefits of "venting". (See below re venting). Instead, when we stay with our confusion, or use our anger as a flag or signal that there is something deeper and more important to deal with, we are in a better position to delay behaviors organized by anger. We are then practicing the thinking that can bolster the neural networks that can increasingly tame the amygdala. We are better able to use our fuller intelligence to better deal with others' behaviors and other events. The Stoic philosopher and playwright, Seneca, said "The greatest remedy for anger is delay."

About venting. In his book *On Aggression*, the ethnologist Konrad Lorenz introduced us to the "psycho-hydraulic" model of human aggression. We often trace back the benefits of "getting your anger out" to this model. However, it's more complicated to actually achieve the assumed benefits of venting. During my time at a residential treatment center, I once observed a teenage girl punching on a body bag to "get her anger out". The more she punched, the angrier she became. When I realized that her knuckles were bleeding, I stopped her and realized that the business of venting was more complicated than I realized, more complicated than popularly thought. Given all the venting taking place in the world today, one might imagine that world peace should be just around the corner. Clearly, venting can be beneficial but as Suzie Pileggi Pawelski and James Pawelski wrote recently in *Psychology Today* about the complications with venting, "Understand *all* emotions are valid and useful. Remember that negative emotions serve a purpose and help us grow. Don't completely ignore or bury them. Instead, channel emotions like anger and sadness to perhaps fight against injustice or reflect on a loss."

Informational Problems. Although the aforementioned problems generally can't be solved without changing underlying thoughts, it should be mentioned that some problems are related to lousy information or a lack of information. A belief in the wrong information can cause problems. Unless one is psychically invested in a belief, informational problems can be comparatively easy to solve. Knowing this is important for all of us but maybe especially for therapists since they have a tendency to not be very good at knowing when *not* to do therapy (let alone when to stop).

A friend once told me a story about a problem that has become my favorite story about an informational problem, a type of problem that can be resolved with information alone. When she was a very young child playing in her backyard one lovely sunny day, she was sitting in the grass chipping away at a rock with a hammer when a beautiful butterfly landed on the rock. She was delighted with the visitation and proceeded to hit the butterfly with her hammer, destroying the butterfly. She was devastated and began to cry uncontrollably. She ran into the house blubbering the story to her mother through her tears. Her mother had the presence of mind to calmly inform her that "we don't hit butterflies with hammers". Future problems solved.

Bottom line. Whenever you're feeling big anger or little anger about anything, or just cranky without a known precipitating event, remember that it's about *you*. Then try to figure out what the expectation was that triggered it. You are then able to examine that trigger and learn about yourself. By practicing this, you will have accomplished one of the most fundamental, if not *the* most fundamental, tasks of psychotherapy. That won't necessarily be a substitute for taking the risk of therapy, but it will give you a head start and likely save you a lot of time and money.

So, whether due to inaccurate or missing information, thoughts due to childhood experiences, or the loss of a known or unrecognized expectation, a change in thinking can lead us to a better outcome.

> "Our world as we have created it is a process of our thinking.
>
> It cannot be changed without changing our thinking."
>
> —Albert Einstein

Chapter 5
More on Feelings Expression
Managing & "Eliminating" Anger

"Give sorrow words: the grief that does not speak

whispers the o're-fraught heart, and bids it break."

–Malcolm to Macduff, *Macbeth*, Act IV, Scene iii

Implications for expressing feelings. When Gert told me that my wife didn't "make me feel" but rather it was me that created my feelings, I mentioned that I was confused and thought that the implication meant I had no recourse in expressing myself when I felt angry or misunderstood. In Chapter 1, I mentioned I wasn't ready for that lesson. But after months of practicing letting go of acting on those feelings and instead just focused on myself and the reasons and expectations that created them, I finally asked Gert "You mean there's nothing I can do but accept the perceived nonsense of others and just put up with it, not assert myself in the face of things I objected to, things I don't think are right?" Gert looked at me almost surprised and talked to me about what we have come to know as "I-messages" even though she didn't use that phrase.

Thomas Gordon, an American psychologist, coined the "I-Message" term in the '60s. His was an important contribution because it helped give us a language for expressing how we feel without necessarily facilitating a defensive response from the person we're talking to by triggering that person's amygdala due to language that attributes culpability for one's feelings to someone else. Rather, it triggers a different part of the brain thought to be the anterior insular cortex.

Other parts of the brain may play a role in empathic response, too, including the amygdala... but the complexity of the mechanism of action here baffles my prefrontal cortex. Suffice it to say, when the anterior insular cortex is activated we are less likely to have a defensive response. For instance, if someone criticizes us and instead of defending ourselves, we agree and empathize with them, saying something like "Thanks for the feedback. I understand what you're thinking. I got myself pretty stretched over that and didn't mean to judge you.", then the person we're talking to is much more likely to reply in an empathetic way and say "That's ok, I may have overreacted, too."

As mentioned before, we don't have a language that we're used to for expressing our feelings of irritation. We get good at what we practice and we are generally much more practiced at being judgmental. In fact, it seems sometimes to be a cultural imperative — that we're expected to tell someone that we're pissed at them, as if that's a righteous behavior. It's as if we have an obligation to "set the person straight".

We are generally told that there is nothing wrong with anger, that it's a natural, normal feeling that is only a problem if it's not expressed in a socially appropriate manner. So as long as we don't "act out" our anger in a violent manner or one that's demeaning to others, it's all good. However, I've never experienced or seen irritated criticism be "pro-social", i.e., promote sociability. It seems rather to promote defensiveness, hurt, and disconnection. If you examine your own reaction to criticism you'll likely realize you've had the same experience.

Structure of an "I-Statement" (See *Problem Solving Protocol — personal* or *inter- & intra-agency* in the Appendix). There are many suggested formats for an I-message available online. Experiment with them or you might try this one: "I heard you say (or thought I saw) *x*", "I thought *y*", "So I got myself feeling *z*", maybe followed by "Thought I'd better see you for a perception check". End of statement. Don't talk too much. For a number of reasons, it's a challenge to talk like this. It's cumbersome, unfamiliar, and sounds weird. But like anything else, the more we do it the easier it flows.

By the way, it's eye-roll hilarious when you see a conscientious person trying hard to talk to someone directly about a concern s/he has without using some version of an I-message. Because we're not used to having the assurance to speak directly to people about concerns, we have with them, nor having the language to do it, the person will carefully hem and haw and try "nicely" to confront somebody about what they perceive as a problem or impropriety. Of course, this type of "careful" attempt tends to telegraph that a shoe is about to drop and sets up a defensive reception before the fact. Even more hilarious are attempts at using I-messages where all the person does is put an "I" in front of an otherwise accusatory statement. "I feel you're being a jerk right now."

I was sitting on a back porch with a friend of mine one afternoon while he was inventing non-lethal weapons for war. I suggested a feelings cannon. I assumed everyone would scatter when they saw expressed feelings coming their way.

Hey, it's hard to tell someone how you're making yourself feel. And it's even more difficult to *receive* expressed feelings. For as often as a therapist may encourage people to talk about how they feel, very little is said about how one should receive those expressions. Maybe this is an additional reason why my inter- & intra-agency problem-solving protocol didn't seem to be appreciated. During my time as clinical director at the day treatment center, and as a privately contracted consultant and supervisor to a few other local agencies, I was under the direction of at least seven different executive directors. The only time the Problem Solving Protocol (PSP) was followed was when I was the clinical director and had the authority to implement it with the clinicians I supervised. That did not include any of the executive directors, or any non-clinical staff under someone else's authority or supervision. The PSP was consistent with the personnel grievance policies for all those agencies. Interestingly, while none of the executive directors codified it specifically into their agency's grievance procedures, they didn't follow it themselves let alone insist that their own middle managers follow the *existing* grievance procedures that required workers to talk to each other directly if they perceived a problem with the other. It was, instead, triangulation that seemed to be codified operationally. (See Chapter 7 regarding assumption-making and "triangulation".) Someone once showed the protocol to a consulting psychiatrist and the consultant was reported to have said "this is very good". I thought he was competent, of course, but that could be a biased evaluation. :^) Nonetheless, two responses I got from executive directors of large agencies were more memorable. I had put copies in their in-house mailboxes as an FYI. One of them never responded so when I saw him one day in passing, I asked if he'd received it. "Oh, yes." he replied, "That's what we do here." I had the opportunity on several occasions to eyewitness that that was *not* what they did there. From him, that response wasn't particularly surprising, but the response from the other exec was. I received her reply back in my box with a little post-it note on the returned PSP that said, "Wouldn't it be nice". I thought it an odd response from the very person who had the authority to turn the Protocol into required policy.

What's So Special About Expressing Feelings? I mean, really? Is that necessary? Heinz Kohut's book *How Does Analysis Cure?* explores the "talking cure" and other aspects of psychoanalysis. Kohut was an Austrian-born American psychoanalyst and professor at the University of Chicago. He is known for developing the influential school of thought called Self Psychology, which focuses on how external relationships shape self-concept and self-esteem. I would recommend reading Kohut for a more in-depth and scholarly assessment of the benefits and origin of "talk therapy". My own thoughts on why the expression of feelings is important is primarily experiential, both personally and professionally.

Because humans rather naturally attempt to avoid pain, it's common and understandable why we wouldn't want to talk about the feelings and memories that are uncomfortable or traumatic. I've had many clients state matter-of-factly that their main strategy for dealing with those kinds of experiences and the emotions attached to them is to not think about them. More than one client has said "Oh, I don't think about it. I just keep those feelings down." Hmm... down where? My friend, Russ Carpenter, once wrote "What you can't deal with doesn't pass. It sinks."

Jessica Jones is a Marvel character from the miniseries by the same name. She's not a touchy-feely gal but has a good heart. When trying to give advice to a traumatized friend, she allowed "They say that talking about a trauma helps, that and jogging, two things that make me feel like crap." Whether or not those two activities, especially talking about trauma, are initially a challenge, and they usually are, it's good advice. (John Briere, a professor emeritus of psychiatry & the behavioral sciences reminds us not to forget that trauma treatment "causes pain".)

When working with children I used my white board to draw primitively silly stick figures with big round bellies. (See Diagram 3.) I would tell them unexpressed feelings don't actually disappear. They stay inside us and show up in disguised forms, examples of which I might list on my whiteboard. (Depending on the client, my list tended to be strategic in that they were designed to capture some of the issues or behaviors for which the child had been referred.) Examples might include anger, fighting, and sadness.[5]

Diagram 3

I would fill the belly circle of the stick figure with a dark color to represent the feelings that were hidden away in the body. I would explain that talking out loud to a non-judging third person could dissipate those dark feelings. As I used my fingers to erase the dark ink, I told them that I didn't really understand how it worked, because I didn't, so I said it was kinda like magic. Honestly, I don't pretend to understand why thinking about how you feel isn't as beneficial as expressing those same dark thoughts out loud through speech. But I do know that talking it out is more challenging and that one needs a safe (confidential, non-judgmental, and empathetic) context in which to do it.

Interestingly, the most hackneyed phrase associated with therapists when conducting therapy is "How does that make you feel?" The attempt to increase a client's awareness of feeling states is worthwhile. But as familiar as we are with the admonition to "express your feelings", it is striking how difficult this can be for us to do it. And frankly, therapists often don't appreciate the degree of the challenge. In order for someone to express their feelings, they first have to be aware that there are feelings there to be expressed. When a therapist suggests to a child or adult that they have such feelings, there's an assumption that the person is aware of what the unexpressed feelings are. Helping someone "get in touch" with those feelings can be no small task. Regardless, as indicated above, expressing feelings out loud to a third party in a safe context has empirically been demonstrated to be beneficial. But to encourage feelings being put into words with the patterned language of a stale cliché, let alone with an inaccurate phrase that attributes those feelings to external factors, isn't very imaginative and certainly isn't "clean", i.e., free from foreign or extraneous matter. (See the reference to "search mode" and patterned language in Chapter 7.)

After trying all this self-discovery stuff, do I still have to put up with people that, for me, are toxic? I don't recommend it. Focusing on anger control, understanding the loss of unmet expectations, calming, use of I-messages, meditation, or even forgiveness (see below), doesn't mean you have to endure people whose presence isn't healthy for you. Just because certain aspects of others mirror something in yourself that is yours to deal with doesn't mean you are required to be around it. Gert even told me once that I wasn't *required* to maintain relationships with members of my family of origin. We may all have relationally challenging people in our lives with whom, for one reason or another, we choose to associate with... and with others we don't associate. Regardless, it is a choice, and most of these relationships represent something within us that is a good idea to explore. Relationships that are important to us are particularly important to explore, maybe especially love relationships with a partner.

My own efforts, described in Chapter 1, were rewarded with the most important personal and professional lessons of my life as well as a wonderful marriage. But the marriage reward had as much to do with the person who was my wife as it was with me. But in my professional experience, the efforts of this same process are identical to what is needed to determine when a relationship *isn't* going to work for you. I don't know how one figures out which relationships have the potential for success without going through the process. The personal variables each person brings to a relationship are too varied to quantify in the search for the "right" person. Despite the outcome of the efforts described in Chapter 1, one is always rewarded with the growth that comes with self understanding. 2,500 years ago Socrates said, "Know thyself". There's still wisdom in this suggestion.

Regarding subsequent troublesome relationships that bear similarities to past ones, I'm inclined to view this as having to do with not learning the lessons for oneself that can only be found within each of us. For instance, if you're entangled in an abusive relationship, there are many very challenging lessons to learn about oneself in order to not find yourself trapped in the same relational situation in your next relationship. But these lessons can only be learned by introspection. Life is very forgiving with respect to giving repeated opportunities to learn specific lessons. (See *The Rules For Being Human* in this Chapter and in the handout Appendix.) If someone tells you that you're in a relationship that needs to be dissolved, whether or not you accept and act on the advice, it will not change the pattern in the future without embarking on a journey of self-exploration. We simply can't see past the level of our own self-development no matter how accurate the outside advice.

A very competent up and coming therapist that I was supervising taught me this. She described a toxic, abusive marriage she'd been in. She went to see a therapist. During the process, the therapist told her she needed to get out of the relationship. The advice was accurate but it wasn't her time, she wasn't ready. She hadn't yet experienced, or learned for herself, the lessons needed to leave her husband. It was *her* journey to find the right path for herself. And it was inadvisable for the therapist to tell her to do so rather than facilitating *her* journey to discover the truths she needed to find. Not feeling understood, she left therapy. Later, she left her husband when it was *her* time to do so. Years later she became one of the best therapists in the county.

A Word on Forgiveness. There's a funny but poignant scene in a Tyler Perry film between a mother and abused daughter where the daughter, now separated from her husband, is struggling to deal with his longstanding abusive behaviors. The mother delivers an offhanded quip that the daughter should forgive her husband. The daughter is shocked and outraged at the mother's suggestion. The mother responds, "You don't forgive because of him, you forgive because of *you*!" Captured in the scene is the idea that forgiveness is a process of escaping the power that the behavior of the perpetrator continues to have over the survivor. The popular connotation of the process of forgiveness seems to evoke an image of talking or writing to the wrongdoer, and of somehow accepting or condoning an injustice. The "act" of forgiveness is actually a process that takes place over time in progressive "scenes". The process has to do with letting go, and overcoming the hurt inflicted by another, letting go of resentment, shame, and the justifiable emotions associated with the wrongdoing. It has to do with having compassion for the wrongdoer even though their behavior has not entitled them to it. It has to do with releasing yourself. It doesn't necessarily have to do with, or require, a reconciliation of the relationship. It doesn't have to do with forgetting or condoning the injustice. It's a process that takes place within you and doesn't even have to be done directly with the person you're forgiving.

Validating Feelings. Most of us have some understanding about the importance of validating feelings, that emotional experience is neither right nor wrong, it just is. Unlike the underlying thoughts or beliefs upon which feelings are predicated and which may be false or inaccurate, feelings are just feelings. Hence, we say they are "valid". Validating the feelings expressed by others is therefore important in the process of empathizing with others and empathetic feedback from others is crucial to our sense of feeling understood and connected in the world and to the relationships that are important to us. Human beings care much more about being *understood* than they do about others being in *agreement* with them.

If, for instance, you explain your position or belief to someone and their response clearly communicates that they understand you but then tell you that they have a different opinion, you are much more likely to listen to their opinion than to argue with them. As explained earlier, being understood registers in the empathy-activating parts of our brain rather than in the parts that activate defensiveness. However, despite our understanding that it's important to validate and empathize with another's feelings, it appears that this is a very difficult thing to do in daily practice, especially when troubling emotions come from the people we love and care about. For example, if your child comes to you in distress, you are likely to feel compelled to immediately relieve their distress, especially if you have information that could help them understand that if they *thought* about the matter differently they could then *feel* differently and be relieved of their troubled feelings. The problem is that if you don't first express empathy and understanding for their emotions, you are likely to get the response "You don't understand!" But empathizing with the distressing feelings of someone we care about can sound kind of lame or inadequate in the face of our desire to be helpful, e.g., "Hmm... that sounds awful." Or "Oh, Gosh, I'm so sorry that's happened."

Nonetheless, if we empathize first, we are more likely to engage with the person, encourage understanding, and facilitate the child or adult to keep talking and continuing their expressing him/herself. Talking out feelings is helpful, acting out feelings can be a problem. Once engaged, the person is more likely to be open to your advice later in the conversation after the emotions are calmed. (See *Two Ideas to Encourage* [Children's] *Self-Esteem* in Appendix)

This unwitting habit we have of not empathizing first is no less likely to happen in adult-to-adult interaction. The additional habit of initially using brief, perfunctory attempts at empathizing are usually just as useless. "Yes, but...." or "I know, but...." This has been referred to as "fly-by" empathy. (See the useful, innovative, evidence-based and trauma-informed work of Stuart Ablon, Ross Greene, and Bruce Perry.) But again, practice makes perfect.

Beyond Anger Management. The most well-known format for anger control is "anger management". The value and benefits provided individually and by anger management groups over the years have been truly helpful. But is it really the state of the art? The phrase itself (if not some of the methods) suggest that the best we can do is "manage" this "natural", "normal" emotion, especially as long as we do it in a "pro-social" way. To me this conjures up the image of a guy sitting in a chair, seething with anger and struggling not to lash out violently while "managing" his anger. When we see that kind of restrained anger we think "Whoa! Dude, you need some anger management." After all, that's exactly what I requested from my therapist years ago only to be told that anger was a "bag of wind". Anger was certainly an ill wind that blew me no good. Hopefully this book has previously described the rationale and methods that can be employed to not only better manage our emotions but to reduce their intensity if not eliminate some of them before they have their way with us.

Self-Congruence with Personal Values. This business of creating and being responsible for your feelings infers that you are not responsible for the feelings of others. And guess what? You're not. In a world where we are frequently accused of hurting someone else's feelings, this is good news. But it also begs the question: "You mean I can act like I want and just blow off the person that says I hurt their feelings?" Nope. You're not on good ground to say "Sorry, honey, that's your problem." The premise of this book doesn't give you a license to be a jerk. Even though it's common to hear people accuse each other of hurting one another's feelings, it's logically not true. We do come by the idea (that others hurt our feelings) honestly in that it's been socialized into us from an early age. I thought once about titling this book "You Don't Know How That Hurts Your Mother!".

Except maybe for those challenged with the personality organization termed "sociopathic narcissist", most of us are socialized with pro-social values. In fact, although I'm not competent to describe it, there are parts of the modern Homo Sapiens' brain that are wired for getting along and living in social groups. Hence, we have values that, through socialization, we've adopted and have come to believe in. When we act in a manner consistent with these values we tend to feel good about ourselves. When we don't, we tend to feel guilty or at least vaguely troubled. Regardless of whether you're not technically responsible for hurting someone's feelings, you're still obligated to be true to the values you say you believe in. One of my own life tasks is to try and live with ever-increasing congruence between my behaviors and my values. When someone misinterprets an intention or behavior, it's still useful to wonder for yourself what the use value might be in the negative feedback you've been given. Even if most of it was misplaced, if even

10% is true, it can be applied as a lesson for future behavior. Every little bit helps.

Speaking of Lessons. Many years ago I stumbled across *The Rules For Being Human* — a catchy title that struck me as humorous and provoking of skepticism. Then I read "The Rules" and was even more struck by the truth they captured and which my own experience had validated. I didn't care for Rule #9 until I'd forgotten about The Rules only to rediscover them later in a file and began using them as a handout for some of my clients. (See below and in the Appendix.) There's a saying that is often met with much derision: "everything happens for a reason". A close friend wrote "Life is random and full of missed turns, bad choices, and stray bits of good luck." Of course it is. The derision is understandable. The phrase is usually interpreted as suggesting life events are preordained. However, we tend to have patterns of behavior. Sometimes these patterns influence a pattern of repeating outcomes in our lives. Sometimes they don't. Regardless, when life events are used to learn how we can better negotiate the inevitable challenges, we can do better than, as my friend, Marco, images as a "helpless wood chip being carried along on life's currents." Insisting on the choice of free will, we are able to assert ourselves along the path of making meaning.

The Rules for Being Human

1. You Will Receive A Body – You may like it or hate it, but it will be yours for the entire period.

2. You Will Learn Lessons – You are enrolled in a full-time informal school called Life. Each day in this school you have the opportunity to learn lessons. If you can actually recognize the opportunity, you may like the lessons or think them irrelevant and hence choose to ignore them, no matter, keep reading.

3. A Lesson Is Repeated Until Learned – A lesson will be presented to you in various forms until you have learned it. When you have learned it, you can then go on to the next lesson.

4. There Are No Mistakes, Only Lessons – Growth is a process of trial and error; experimentation. The "failed" experiments are as much a part of the process as the experiment that ultimately "works".

5. Learning Lessons Does Not End – There is no part of life that does not contain its lessons. If you are alive, there are lessons to be learned.

6. "There" Is No Better Than "Here"– When your "there" has become a "you" will simply obtain another "there" that will, again, look better than "here".

7. Others Are Merely Mirrors Of You – You cannot love or hate something about another person unless it reflects to you something you love or hate about yourself.

8. Your Answers Lie Only Inside Of You – The answers to Life's questions lie only inside of you. All you need to do is look, listen, and trust.

9. You Will Forget All This

—Anonymous

"Life is a succession of lessons

which must be lived to be understood."

—Helen Keller

Chapter 6
More on Anger
Moron Anger

"A quick temper will make a fool of you soon enough."

—Bruce Lee

Prior to the year 2000, there hasn't been a great deal of research on anger compared to studies on anxiety and depression. For instance, according to Tal Ben Shahar from Harvard University, between the mid-'60s and the year 2000, there were roughly 54,000 psychological abstracts regarding depression, approximately 41,500 about anxiety, and only about 4,500 having to do with anger... and even less on joy and happiness. More recently this has changed somewhat (See Jennifer Lerner, et. al. Harvard University) but anger is still understudied and arguably misunderstood.

If you search online for the "benefits of anger" or "positive" aspects of anger, you'll get a number of hits. For example, from the Amen Clinics (See Daniel Amen, MD) you'll run across an article titled "*6 Surprising Benefits of Anger*". As with many of these articles, it's easy to simply construe that anger is beneficial. After all, amygdala activation certainly had adaptive significance for the survival of Homo Sapiens and does indeed alert us to danger or underlying issues for which it would be wise to be aware. An excerpt from this article reads "Anger can serve as an opportunity for spiritual and emotional growth. Anger can be an indication that there's a deeper issue that needs to be addressed. A willingness to look at the source of our anger can be beneficial. Being both curious about, and constructive in, exploring our anger can provide insight into our faults and shortcomings, and lead to character development and greater self-esteem".

Another excerpt from this same article reads "Anger provides us with a sense of control and corresponding optimism. Anger propels us to use our individual power, alone or collectively, to inflict costs or withhold benefits to get what we need. Individuals who constructively experience and express their anger are in a better position to fulfill their needs and control their destiny than those who suppress their anger." In my opinion, these research-based statements are not inaccurate but nonetheless require careful examination — examination of what "opportunity" means or what is meant by "constructively experience and express [one's] anger".

Otherwise, these articles can be misconstrued and result in confusion and the reinforcement of the more popular thinking that "there's nothing wrong with anger", "it's natural". (It's probably "organic" and gluten-free but that doesn't mean it's good for you.)

I would hope that the previous chapters in this book could be helpful in guiding the aforementioned process of examining anger so that it serves as an alert to the personal, underlying feelings that can, though sometimes painful to deal with, lead to greater control, understanding, and satisfaction.

This hope is arguably a timely one in the era this book is written. The rise of anger and belligerence in popular culture is obvious. (See Jeffrey Fleishman's LA Times article *How an Angry National Mood is Reflected in Pop Culture*)

"Anger" in Sports Broadcasts. Although the upswing in cultural anger is a serious issue, I find myself shaking my head and giggling at the current use or application of the word "anger" by broadcast sports commentators or sports participants who often seemingly promote the benefits of anger by use of the phrase "playing angry". One of my sons-in-law recently mentioned that there's even a new NFL football show called *Angry Runs* which highlights the best running plays of the week. Playing with "anger" and "violence" are now both common catchwords. My wife suggested that playing with "focus and finesse" might be more effective. A longtime college basketball sports analyst commenting on how a National title contender needed to play in the second half said "They're gonna have to play angry." Another well-known football commentator advised one team to play with "controlled rage", an oxymoron to be sure. Given how anger and rage affect the brain's prefrontal cortex they might as well have said "they're gonna have to play stupid".

Prior to a recent NASCAR playoff race, one of the commentators said drivers were going to need to be "fueled with frustration and anger" in order to be competitive. The idea of being frustrated and angry while driving at 180+ mph doesn't seem to be prudent advice. We already have evidence that at 70 mph on an interstate freeway road rage has undesirable consequences.

As I write this, one of the Oregon college football teams is playing their biggest game of the year. One of Oregon's premier wide receivers angered himself. Here's an excerpt from a fake news article that was never written:

"The Ducks were already underdogs before they lost their best defensive player in practice last week. Then, early in the game, a defender in Ohio State's secondary had the audacity to make one of Oregon's premier wide receivers mad. With his amygdala activated and his prefrontal cortex having lost as many as 30 points, he decided it was a good idea to spit in the face of the defender that pissed him off. Oddly, the officials were not impressed by the receiver's being temporarily rendered stupid. They penalized Oregon 15 yards for unsportsmanlike conduct and then ejected the receiver from the game." Stupid is as stupid does. Biblically, Ecclesiastes 7:9 reminds us "Be not quick in your spirit to become angry, for anger lodges in the heart of fools."

Regarding anger, the famed martial artist, Bruce Lee, reminds us with his quote above of the well understood importance of focus when competing in sports but it seems the misunderstood emotion of anger has seeped into the culture and is becoming more commonplace. It's likely also true that some of these commentators could be referring to the benefits of anger in the same way that the Amen Clinics' article above describes but *how* to use that energy to focus and motivate is not delineated by these analysts when advising participants to "play angry".

In keeping with Bruce Lee's wisdom, it certainly isn't true that all sports figures are unaware of the pitfalls of emotional reactions. Just today a premier NFL running back was being asked about the big game they lost a year ago and what he thought about "having a score to settle" in the upcoming game with the same team. It was a pretty transparent sports journalist question likely designed to tap into the emotions that might be attached to an assumed need for revenge. But instead of some paybacks-are-a-bitch response the running back said "I don't really think about that. It's best not to let emotions overcome focus." Likewise, when an Indianapolis 500 interviewer asked former Indy 500 winner Scott Dixon if the stress of starting on the pole is greater than starting further back on the qualifying grid, Dixon replied "Well, stress is something you do to yourself." Dixon has won the Indycar Series six times.

Culture & Politics. In a more widespread context I wrote earlier that in regard to anger and being judgmental "it seems sometimes to be a cultural imperative." That reference regarding the use of the emotion of anger in sports is, it seems, reflective of a cultural phenomenon in general. In the last several years there has been an uptick in articles that express concern about the increase in anger in America's mood.

Much has been written as to *why* this is the case. Some point to the rise in conspiracy theories, others attribute this to the popularity of social media and the protection it provides in saying things that would otherwise be said with more moderation if talking in more personal, social contexts. Others suggest that many things have simply gotten worse, like the decline in manufacturing jobs in the last two decades. Nonetheless, there is little evidence for these as causative factors regarding the increase in our collective anger. For instance, contrary to popular opinion, many of these factors have actually been pretty stable and there is evidence that many things have improved. For example, prior to the Covid pandemic in 2020 unemployment had reached historic lows, income equality has risen in the last three decades (although middle class incomes are down compared to the top 1%), non-managerial workers' wages are up significantly since 2000, Crime rates have fallen since the 1990s, and poverty has declined.

There is some evidence to suggest that bias in journalism has something to do with this polarization. But regardless of the reasons, "affected polarization", defined as the phenomenon where people's feelings and emotions towards members of their own political party or group become more positive, while their feelings towards members of the opposing party or group become more negative, has clearly increased significantly and public trust in government and many of its institutions have eroded significantly since the year 2000 (See Pew Research Center).

At the time of this writing, I knew many reasonable and thoughtful people, who consumed various sources of news who said, "I don't know what to believe", as if their individual ability to discern facts and be wary of cognitive distortion as might arise from confirmation bias, has suddenly and mysteriously been co-opted. Someone once said, "The truth is out there, way out there." But the belief that we no longer have the ability to determine the closest approximation of the truth is as disheartening as it is inaccurate.

Be that as it may, none of these suggestions that might explain the increase in the cultural anger, including the research that supports these suggestions, delves into the *why* of the why, i.e., what it is that may lie deeper than the secondary emotion of anger. Or, given the previously described Anger-Loss model, what is the loss? What are the primary feelings of the heart that might be more challenging and painful to uncover?

In 2024 APM Research Lab conducted a study regarding the United States' mood, *Mood of the Nation: Angry*. Not surprisingly, the questions the study asked were consistent with the popular phraseology upon which the premise of this book is based and from which the title is derived: the discrepancy between what we say and what the source of our emotions actually are. For example, "*What is there about American politics today that makes you feel ANGRY?*" My point isn't to suggest that they should have used more accurate phraseology. But if they had, it might've been representative of a different cultural norm that could better remind all of us of the actual locus of control of our emotions and feelings.

My point is that research, like most everything else, is reflective of the culture and not necessarily apart from it. In the same sense, there is no such thing as "pure" science — no such thing as being able to think outside the epistemological box in which we reside. It also may represent one of many reasons why survey data isn't particularly reliable. In this case, not only does the use of the popular vernacular reinforce the notion that humans put the control of emotions into the hands of external marionette operators but it also tends to keep us from empowering ourselves with a more useful understanding of how emotions can be changed through the examination of the expectations and feelings from which they're actually derived. (It's not clear to me whether or not using the "shouted" convention of all caps to write the word "ANGER" in the survey question was in itself a form of bias... but don't get me started on the obnoxious and unnecessary shouting that is now commonplace among many sport analysts' TV shows.)

In the matter of our current National mood, I suggest that understanding the profound sense of confusion, sadness and despair about, and disconnection from, our heartfelt National values could provide better guidance toward the type of behaviors that could reduce our current state of anger and intolerance.

Whether or not this understanding could benefit from an examination of a seeming discrepancy between our heartfelt values of equity and concern for others and a primary daily operating value requiring a focus on ideological and material self interest is speculative.

My own face-to-face experiences with people throughout the country is in contradiction with the country's mood. As mentioned before, that which people (from all cultures) have in common is so much more important than the differences we have. I recently took a road trip with my wife. We traveled from California to the Mid-West and back across the northern tier of states to home again. We crossed through many states that are politically labeled red, blue, and purple. (We subconsciously followed the basic pro-social norm of not discussing politics or religion.) Following the trip we realized we were gratified to know that people were people. Our individual interactions with folks were most pleasant. Everyone we met along the way was cordial, friendly, respectful, generous, and helpful when needed.

"Anything which is troubling you,

anything which is irritating you, *that* is your teacher."

—Ajahn Chah

Chapter 7
Other Clinical Practice Insights

"We don't see everything we think we see

because we have a routine way of looking."

—J.W. Moog

Treatment Made Simple. Of course, psychotherapeutic treatment is not simple. But there are some things one can do to help keep a therapist on track amid the complexities of the process. Inasmuch as necessity is the mother of invention, the context of my initial work helped provoke me into finding some methods that helped accomplish more effective "front-end" work with which to lay the foundation for treatment as well facilitating the "simplification" of the challenge.

I began my postgraduate clinical work doing therapy in a private, non-profit psychiatric day treatment center with children (12 and under) and their families. Day treatment is usually, by definition, locally based with children residing with their own families (or with foster families). In this context, the parents were usually best considered as "semi-mandated" in that the children referred were not negotiating the normal public school environment in a minimally adequate manner and as such, not only were the parents having to deal with the reality that their kids weren't making it in the usual setting of public school, but they had to deal with the perceived stigma of agreeing to sending them to a "special school" populated with other emotionally and/or behaviorally troubled peers as well as being somewhat "coerced" by the public school circumstance of being subjected to a bunch of therapists. After relenting to this situation, many of these parents were at least hoping that their children would be "fixed" by attending the program and few imagined that their own participation in their child's therapy was required or necessary. (The idea that the program wasn't a "fix-it" shop but more realistically a "discovery shop" was an added complication.) Once, after introducing myself to a mother as the agency's family therapist, she exclaimed "Oh, thank God!", but this was rare. Since therapists aren't nearly as important to children as their parents are, involvement of the parents was usually crucial.

Arguably, this was the most challenging clinical population in the county. Families that have more monetary wealth, but who also have troubled children, have more opportunities to avoid publicly funded services. In the clinical population of state subsidized nonprofit day treatment, the parents' internal and external resources were not often a strength. To use John Briere's term, their "adaptive resources" were often scant. Engagement into a genuine therapeutic alliance was a challenge. Since my own clinical experience in other postgraduate mental health contexts was also scant at the time, this proved to be an invaluable training ground, even though I wasn't aware of it. (Many years later when I started a private practice, I actually had the thought that I was somehow "cheating" because the context of self-referred clients who were actively seeking therapy was so much different than day treatment, and comparatively easy.)

As alluded to previously, the use of the Self, the primary tool of a therapist, is probably the most important factor in engagement. But since everyone's got a different Self, it would be foolish to try and describe mine, even if I could. Nonetheless, there are some things that help. One of them is how one goes about goal setting.

Treatment goals are one of the most important, common, and basic requirements of developing a professional treatment plan. Although much has been described about this process, from documentation, accountability, and measurement of outcomes, it seems to remain a challenging process, partly because it is often seen, or practiced, as a task of documentation rather than one to be employed in the process of engagement.

As both the sole family therapist in the program and later as the clinical director, I insisted on being the first person to meet with the parents. Although it's more difficult to do this in a large program or clinic, off-loading this initial task to a separate intake-worker or assessment specialist, rather than the therapist who will provide treatment, delays and/or is an obstacle to forming a therapeutic relationship.

After initial introductions, acknowledgment of, and empathy with, the challenges of the situation the parents found themselves in, along with program and role clarifications, goal setting can then begin. Regarding the initial contact, it became a wonderment to me how the use of honesty and straightforwardness could actually be a "technique" in greasing the skids of engagement. Many of these client families had dealt with other social services and schools in the past, including child protective services. As such, they had previous experience with bureaucrats and professionals who frequently and unwittingly get trapped inside the box of the politic speech that passes for professionalism.

Therapists, too, can get unknowingly trapped in the use of a "professional tone" in their speech. When, in my private practice, a client was having trouble with something I was saying, either because of the content or just the unconventional, colloquial manner in which I might be speaking at the time, I might say to them "Well, would you be more comfortable if I talked more like what you imagined would be from a more typical therapist?" Then I would go into an act where I would sit back in my chair, cross my legs, and in a subdued manner ask, "And how did that make you feel?" The client, often a high school kid, would giggle, shake their head, and acquiesce to my manner. Of course, you have to know your client and the type of relationship you have with them in order to risk that kind of lightheartedness. The process of therapy is a serious one. To inject it with humor at appropriate times can be beneficial.

Some of the unnecessary trappings of what passes for professional tone and manner can also inadvertently detract from a therapist's use of empathy. For example, in the meeting with a client who's coming to a therapy session (or introductory meeting at the day treatment center) for the first time, you can tell pretty quickly via body language if the new client is experiencing the normal nervousness and trepidation that most of us feel when going to see a therapist. I mean, really, going to see a therapist is a very strange experience, for all of us. To not recognize this, or address it, is a missed opportunity in the process of engagement. As a therapist I might say "Pretty weird moment, isn't it — coming to see a therapist? It's weird for all of us." And subsequently suggesting "So, it must be something pretty important that got you to come anyway." This kind of recognition can be helpful in getting the conversation and relationship started. The disarming benefits of empathizing with this moment, and *normalizing* it, can be invaluable for the client.

Tangentially, Lynn Johnson refers to the use value of the brain being in "search mode". When people use patterned language, they tend to get patterned responses. When we hear unexpected language, the brain clicks into search mode and is more likely to contemplate what is actually being said. Thus, more thoughtful, novel responses are more likely. It is unfortunate that the alleged "professional" speech of social service workers, therapists, and bureaucrats is often perceived by its consumers as deceptive double-talk... but fortunately, this also means that honest, straightforward, colloquial speech is perceived as unexpected or novel.

In the process of engagement, whether day treatment or private practice, it is imperative to find out the parent(s)' or client(s)' story, what their hopes are and what things would look like (in concrete, behavioral terms) if this process they were risking was to be beneficial. Using non-pathology-based and colloquial language matters. Translating what *they* hope for into simple, lowest denominator goals is important. Assuring your clients that it will be *their* goals that will be the purpose of their involvement also matters. Assuring them that the "pack of therapists" won't, behind their back, be inventing or working on what *they* think the goals should be is not only in keeping with the ethical principle of "client right to self-determination", it is strategic to developing trust and allaying the fear that therapy is a mysteriously coercive process being orchestrated by a mind-reader who "knows what's best".

Explaining to clients before the fact that there will be no arguments about the goals is important. Explaining that the only disagreements or conflicts will be about methods, and that it is the job of the therapist to explain how the methods are in keeping with the goals, or if they can't, it is the therapist's obligation to change the methods so that they are compatible with the goals. In the context of day treatment, methods include listing example practices like psychiatric evaluation, individual child therapy, group therapy, marriage counseling, individual therapy with the adults, child management, and even medication.

It's also important to remember or realize that most all parents want the same things for their children that we all want. We want our children to be happy, to have meaningful, satisfying relationships with others, and for our children to have the skills to negotiate the disappointments and challenges of life.

In this process it's important to explain the responsibilities of the program (or therapist if a private practice). Based on the presenting or referral problems, an assessment must be made. I always explained the assessment as a hypothesis — or a "best guess" as to what might be going on that could explain referral behaviors. Occasionally the parent(s) claimed there was no problem with the child and that inadequacies at the public school or misinterpretation at child protective services was the problem. In those instances I suggested that day treatment was unnecessary and recommended that an attorney be sought. The parent(s) usually reconsidered their position at that point. On only two occasions did the referral process end there. (It is a fool's game to attempt treatment when the basic conditions of treatment are not met.)

Subsequently these "best guess" assessment examples could include a number of things that might explain the reasons for referral, including biochemical or developmental problems, unknown traumas, child management issues, problems in parental relationship, or substance addictions. These examples were written on my whiteboard and were usually strategic "guesses" based on referral information.

Once these goals are established, they must be documented in your intake notes. This is not just for the purpose of translating them accurately into a treatment plan with specified methods and measurable outcome indicators, but for the purpose of meeting with parents later in the therapy process for clarification of treatment purposes, especially when and if things get off track.

The forces of getting off track with this particular clinical population are rather powerful. The previously mentioned drive for "homeostatic equilibrium" mentioned in the beginning of Chapter 3 is formidable, regardless if that equilibrium is maladaptive and sabotaging to a family's goals. The drama, chaos, and crises that seem to be patterns in these families are common and commonly help distract or interfere with what needs to be a goal-directed treatment process. As challenging as this might be for therapists, it also comes with the territory and should be expected. Attempting to get these patterns "out on the treatment table" is as necessary as it is tough. But it's important to recognize and incorporate them into the family's awareness because they will otherwise become examples of the family incorporating the therapist into the family system rather than the therapist facilitating change in that maladaptive system. I've had the thought that families are better at being themselves than therapists are at being therapists.

Narrative Therapy. One of the therapeutic methods that I found to be remarkably helpful in getting a family's or individual's self-sabotaging patterns into client awareness during the treatment process has been through the groundbreaking work of Michael White and David Epston, Australian and New Zealand, respectively, social workers and psychotherapists. Bill O'Hanlon, a noted psychotherapist and educator, wrote an article for *The Psychotherapy Networker* titled "The Third Wave". O'Hanlon, a practitioner of Solution-Focused "brief" therapy credits the work of White and Epston to be as big a leap forward in the therapeutic profession as solution-focused, problem-solving, brief therapy approaches have been to Freudian Psychoanalysis.

I won't try to describe this work in much detail here but will recommend to clinicians that are unfamiliar with White and Epston to check it out. In general, this approach focuses on a model quite different than the classic "medical model" which tends to focus on the expertise of a professional to diagnose the patient and prescribe a treatment — a model that works pretty well for broken and malfunctioning bodies but also lends itself to unwittingly disempower psychotherapy clients from using their own wisdom while it also tends to use pathology-based language that can presume that the client's troubles inherently reside in, or are, the client. For instance, if someone is plagued with anger or a bipolar disorder, we commonly refer to them as "being an angry person" or "being bipolar". Narrative therapy uses language that focuses on the problem as the problem and "externalizes" it from the person. Almost magically, this tends to reduce patterned defenses and frees the client to discuss more openly the behavioral patterns with which they're troubled.

One of the first times I attempted this model I was working with a mom that was forever beset with crises in her life. In her telling of her story, she frequently used the word "chaos". I started asking her "structured questions" in keeping with the model. I first asked, "How long has Chaos been messing with you?" She said "forever". I asked, "What effect has Chaos had in your life and your relationships?" She freely told me and made a reference to it driving her crazy. I asked, "How has Chaos encouraged the Crazy Lifestyle?" She openly discussed various aspects of her life and how she was overwhelmed by it. I asked, "What habits do you have that Chaos encourages?" Contrary to my past interviewing experiences, she freely described many self-sabotaging behaviors. I asked, "What habits might you practice if you wanted to disobey Chaos?" And damned if she didn't then start openly delineating non-self-sabotaging behaviors that her own wisdom already knew about! I was not only stunned at the difference this externalizing language made but this mom had virtually written her own treatment plan for accomplishing her goals. In turn, her subsequent personal efforts to change things at home dovetailed with the overall treatment plan for her child and reduced the crises-induced, multiple sidetracks that otherwise impeded treatment progress.

That this mother already knew the solutions to her troubles was not surprising. There's a thought, spoken or not, among people seeking therapy and among some therapists that therapy is a passive process. Although it sounds silly, the idea that a therapy client will be "therapized" into mental health is not uncommon. But therapists don't "make someone better" any more than teachers do the learning for their students. It's the therapy client that does the work of therapy in the same way that students do the learning. The skill of a teacher or therapist is that of a "process facilitator". I've sometimes thought of a therapist as being like an "interactive mirror" who reflects back the internal wisdom already within the client's subconscious awareness. An experienced therapist that I once worked with similarly referred to this as "working to the side" of the client, making suggestions "obliquely" in an effort to kindle the client's own internal knowledge rather than trying to "extract" a client's problems. When Macbeth was demanding that the court physician "Pluck from the memory a rooted sorrow" out of Lady Macbeth's brain, the doctor replied, "Therein the patient must minister to himself." (*Macbeth*, Act V, Scene iii)

Pathology-Based Thinking. The above story of this mother also tended to reinforce an idea I had — the idea that because their children were the most important thing in their lives, "bad parents" were actually much more rare than suggested by the common use of this phrase. Most parents try their best to make things better. Even stupid and egregious behaviors are attempts to change things despite many of those behaviors having a tendency to be destructive and to keep things the same. The corollary is even more provocative: the idea that "people do the best they can" ... in the moment of the doing of it. This is a phrase that is often met with as much derision as "everything happens for a reason". But that's not to say they couldn't do better. Nonetheless it's pretty rare for parents or individuals to wake up in the morning trying to figure out what they need to do during the day to make their lives worse, to mess up their kids, or themselves, or how to get other people to not like them. Regardless, it's more productive to acknowledge to parents that their motivation and efforts are not in question but rather that their energy to make things better might be more productive if it was *repackaged* in a different form.

The advent of "strategic family therapies" in the late 60s and 70s gave rise to the notion that dysfunction within families served a purpose. Typically, these had to do with maintaining homeostatic equilibrium, albeit usually in maladaptive ways. Hence, family therapists were asking the question "What purpose does this dysfunction serve?" I'm not suggesting there wasn't (and isn't) merit to this question or this type of thinking. But it wasn't very useful to me, maybe because it required too much conjecture about the complexities within family dynamics but also, for me, it seemed to require too much pathology-based thinking. I was better off having my mind organized by what was already working in a family, what their survival strengths were and to help them focus on how they had already survived so many challenges. Going to see a therapist wasn't a sign of failure — it was just another attempt to make things better. It was easier for me to think that dysfunctional dynamics served primarily to oppress families. The analogy of the cooked frog made more sense to the simplicity of my own mind. In the analogy to a family, a frog is put into a pot of water on a stove and the temperature is degree by degree turned up in discrete increments so that the frog has time to adapt to each increase. Although the frog adapts, it is eventually cooked. Solution/problem-focused models were easier for me in helping families reduce the heat.

It's not my intention to make the assumption that the thinking in the above paragraph works for all practitioners. It just worked for me.

"What?!... *Me* Make Assumptions?" Marge, the town gossip and supervisor of the town's morals, told Rodney that Ray was an alcoholic. She told Rodney that she had seen Ray's car last night, parked in front of the only bar in town and it was still there the next morning. Rodney nodded his head slightly but didn't say anything. That evening Rodney parked his car in front of Marge's house and left it there all night.

Although most everyone is familiar with the adage "That to assume makes an '*ass* of *u* and *me*'", this knowledge is a challenge to put into daily practice. If, as stated previously in Chapter 4, "Expectations are the root of all evil" then assumptions are one of the primary feeder tendrils in that rootball.

One of my most important lessons was learning how *not* to pay attention to second-hand information. This can be quite a challenge when that information comes in a heartfelt manner from a trusted friend or colleague. But nonetheless, second-hand information about a third party that doesn't represent the *truth* of your *own* experience with that same person is best ignored. What's come to be known as "triangulation" is a common and usually useless process. Person A tells person B about some impropriety committed by person C. Person B goes to person C and confronts them on the assumption that person A's information is true. Almost inevitably person C says "that's not true" or otherwise gives a different story with different circumstances. Person B is then in a dilemma and all three people are vexed. You can test this for yourself by recalling your own experiences with triangulation whether you played the role of person A, B, or C. This troublesome type of interaction happens in personal as well as professional relationships.

In professional organizations, and despite personnel policies that supposedly require co-worker concerns to be taken up with that fellow worker directly as a first step in the grievance process, a disgruntled worker may go directly to their supervisor (who should be available initially for "venting" but not direct action.) The supervisor may then go directly to the worker who's being implicated. It's a dumb but common practice. In that situation it's all too rare, after venting, for the supervisor to direct their supervisee back to the worker who's being complained about.

I was once involved in an interesting if not comical situation regarding assumptions and triangulation. I was doing contract clinical supervision for a county's child & family therapist team. One of my supervisees was doing contract work in a public school. (The therapist I was supervising happened to be very competent and professional.) She was troubled and confused by the fact that a teaching assistant employed by the school had apparently complained about her to the assistant's immediate supervisor. That supervisor informed her supervisor about the complaint. That supervisor contacted her managerial counterpart at the county mental health department. The counterpart supervisor then contacted my supervisee's immediate supervisor whereupon the therapist informed me of the complaint. After explaining the process of triangulation (akin to "strangulation") and pointing out how this process was also contrary to the personnel grievance policies stated for both organizations, I told her to inform her immediate supervisor what I had said and to have her supervisor send the "complaint" back down the circuitous path from which it came. Unsurprisingly, that was the last the therapist heard of the matter. (See *Problem Solving Protocol, inter- & intra-agency* in the Appendix)

Assumption-making is also a problem in professional practice regarding psychosocial evaluation of clients. Once a diagnosis is made, or a hypothesis as to what's going on is guessed, it's easy to get invested in that initial assessment and to inadvertently assume you happened to have stumbled upon the assessment that will help guide an effective treatment. But the treatment plan is best viewed as a "hypothesis tester". Assessments should be ephemerally ongoing. Therapists aren't paid to be "believers", their obligation is to be professionals and to continually question the possibility of varied etiologic cause. So, for instance, as a first step, writing off a lack of progress in treatment to "client resistance" is simply not professional.

When one's training results in a practitioner's proficiency in a particular area of treatment, there's a tendency to over-diagnose the problems for which you're trained and are effective at treating. Part of the problem with being a "good therapist" who has training in determining causes of behavioral and emotional problems is that we're not particularly well trained in, for example, medical problems, or educational learning disabilities that may manifest in ways similar to the causes of some emotional and behavioral problems... which can in and of themselves be a cause of emotional and behavioral problems. The broader our knowledge and training can be, the less likely we are to mis-evaluate or to not see that a single symptom might be the result of more than one cause. In auto mechanics, the most befuddling problems are two causes of a single symptom at the same time.

The Bed of Procrustes. In Greek mythology Procrustes was a highwayman who preyed upon travelers, robbing them of their merchandise and valuables. He then took the travelers to his cave and laid them out on his stone slab "bed". If they didn't fit the bed exactly he stretched them out if they were too short. Or, if they were too long, he lopped off what was overhanging in order to make them fit. This parable of extremes, so to speak, reminds us of our tendency to fit reality into what we believe in, or what we're trained to see. As humans, we live in a subjective world. Objectivity is a theoretical construct that we may strive for, but inherently fall short of. Being diligent about the ubiquitous nature of assumption-making can be helpful in avoiding these pitfalls.

I will be forever grateful to Bradley Castle, my 10th grade high school biology teacher. Dryly funny, astute, and eccentric, Mr. Castle had a large banner that hung on the wall in the front of his classroom that read "Cautious Judgment". Like everyone else, I'm prone to falling short of his admonition but it was a good early guide for my life and clinical development.

The Primary Parental Dilemma. This dilemma in parenting is commonplace for those of us who love our children, which is to say, most all of us. The dilemma has to do with a parental paradox we inherit when we raise children, one that needs to be adequately resolved for effective parenting. It has to do with the knowledge that we are their primary protectors and advocates. If ***we*** are not there for them, who else would be? It also has to do with knowing we have the obligation to raise them to understand the rules of life's road so they can negotiate the inevitable challenges they will encounter.

We prefer to love our children by giving and providing what they want. Loving them by giving them what they need is more of a challenge. Knowing which to do when is the dilemma, and most of us err on the side of giving them what they want, without necessarily ill effect. But, as with most things, striking the right balance is best.

Prior to the age of one year it is almost impossible to overindulge a child. By the age of two, the parental dilemma emerges. A family therapist, whose name I forget, said that effective parenting requires us to "fail our children" by which he meant not always giving them what they want, not trying to relieve all their distresses, not robbing them of the opportunities to learn their own lessons so that they can develop the skills to negotiate disappointments. (See *The Primary Parental Dilemma* in the Appendix)

Neurological Differences between Men and Women. Over the last 20 years neuroscience has contributed a better understanding of how the use value of certain psychotherapeutic practices has been corroborated by neurology and brain function. The often controversial subject of neurological differences between men and women has been as enlightening as it has been contradictory. (See *Neurosexism: the myth that men and women have different brains* in Nature.com; *Two Minds* from stanmed .stanford.edu; and *Male and Female Brains* in www.Psychologytoday)

What we know for sure is that there are differences for clinicians and laypeople to be aware of because of their explanatory benefits. But since socialization and cultural differences over thousands of years also play a role, what percentage we give to the differences regarding nature vs. nurture is unknown and likely doesn't matter for the purpose here.

There's some evidence in the neuroscience literature suggesting that men are better wired for perception and motor skills while women are better wired for multi-tasking, intuitive thinking, and are likely to have better analytical skills as well as being more tuned in to operating in relationships. Regarding adaptive significance, this could make some sense when we think of our ancestors' early gender-related tasks such as men hunting in the savanna and being watchful for the Sabertooth while women were more likely to be working at home and caring for children in the company of other women.

Regardless, my own experience, both personally and professionally, regarding these differences is largely anecdotal. Since anecdotal evidence is considerably less reliable than even survey data, I won't test the reader's tolerance with generalizations that I can't support but I will say that my experiences have been as striking as they have been helpful to me and my clients.

During the early part of the marriage to my late wife, I had an experience that was confusing. On a work day when my wife would ask me to pick something up before I came home (like groceries or a household item), or asked me to make a phone call for some domestic reason, I would readily agree. When I got home from work and she asked about her request, which I would routinely forget, she was disappointed. Over time when my forgetting had become a pattern, her disappointment became more exasperated. She didn't directly voice that she questioned my caring about her and the kids but this was certainly on her mind as she tried to explain to herself why I didn't remember to do what I said I'd do. Adding to her concern, and to my confusion, was the fact that when I made similar requests of her, she rarely forgot.

I did, however, care deeply about my wife and family and so began to wonder why this difference between us was the case. Fortunately, even though I had no answers, I guess I was kind of a problem-solving guy. In this process I realized that when I was at work I didn't forget things. I realized that I routinely used props to remember my work tasks. I used to-do lists and I had an appointment book that I regularly referred to. So I began using my appointment book before going to work to write down these domestic requests. No one gets in trouble for having a forgetting problem. We get in trouble for not taking responsibility for having a forgetting problem. In my case, using the prop of my appointment book became useful in taking responsibility for what I would otherwise forget.

It wasn't long after, coincidentally, I was reading an article about differences between men and women. It was fascinating. The author made an analogy of some of these differences by using rooms in a house. He said if the rooms that one would go into represented the different roles that men and women played in their lives, like that of mother, father, worker, lover, shopper, housecleaner, automobile oil-changer, etc., women took the relationships in their lives with them into every room. Men, on the other hand, tended to only take themselves into the room. Men had more of a single-minded focus on the task at hand represented in each room. I read that a corollary to this was that when men and women got into conflicts, women were more likely to think that the man "doesn't care about me and/or the kids — that he doesn't pay attention." Meanwhile, the man who perceived that he tried conscientiously to comply with his wife's expectations tended to think

"No matter what I do, I can't please her – it's never enough, she can't be satisfied." I further read that these differences accounted for 80% of the reasons why couples get divorced. (Sadly, I'm ignorant to what extent any of this might apply to LGBTQ+ couples. As with many areas of research, my guess is that this may be an artifact of how marginalized populations are underserved in general.) This analogy fit with my own experiences, like the forgetting to follow through on the tasks my wife had requested.

I began to use this analogy in my work with couples, and individuals that were complaining about their partners. Strikingly, when I would describe the analogy to individual women clients that I was working with in therapy and told them how they would take their important relationships, like those with their partners and children, into the different rooms of their house, they almost always had a response to the effect "Yeah, so what's your point?" I would go on to tell them, as a man, I don't understand this. I don't do that. They often expressed the same puzzlement about my not thinking like they did as I had about their thinking. It was a revelation to them (as it was to me) that their partner came about these thinking differences "honestly".

Whether talking to women or men, I would go on to say that these differences were not something that in a relationship could be used as excuses for the unwanted behavior in the other. Relationships are by definition a compromise for the individual. With the exception, of course, regarding the "correct" way to hang a roll of toilet paper..., most of the time, there is no evidence for what partners argue is the "right" way to do something (See Brent J. Atkinson, Ph.D.'s *The Love Breakthrough)*. It is, instead, useful for these differences to be taken into account and for partners to take responsibility for having different ways of thinking. In fact, I would suggest that these differences are actually useful to each other in that when accepted in combination, relationships can be richer and more effective since these differences can otherwise compensate for what each type of thinking is lacking.

That said, as to why my wife is right 90-95% of the time, I don't know... but I have accepted it and don't know whether it has to do with any wiring differences in the genders. But in the two wonderful marriages that I have been blessed with in this life, this has been true whenever we've had differences of opinion. I knew a medical doctor who was a generation older than me who once said, "My marriage got better when I finally realized that my wife was right most of the time." :^)

"Statues made of matchsticks,

Crumble into one another,

My love winks, she does not bother,

She knows too much to argue or to judge."

—Bob Dylan

Empty your cup. There's a Zen Buddhist parable that represents the importance of being open to new ideas despite what we think we know or what our operating reality is.

Similarly, Bob Dylan reminds us that "those not busy being born are busy dying." Uncomfortable or not, we create our own reality and to be open to new realities can have rewards. In his brilliant introduction to *Collected Poems*, E. E. Cummings reminds us of the same thing in this excerpt: "...Never the murdered finalities of wherewhen and yesno, impotent nongames of wrongright and rightwrong;never to gain or pause,never the soft adventure of undoom,greedy anguishes and cringing ecstasies of inexistence;never to rest and never to have;only to grow.

Always the beautiful answer who asks a more beautiful question"

———-

A long time ago there was a Zen master who lived somewhere deep in the mountains. People came to him and asked him to teach them. One day a professor made the long journey to visit and asked him for his wisdom. The professor introduced himself to the Zen master by mentioning his academic credentials and then he said: "I have come today to ask you to teach me about Zen. Open my mind to enlightenment." The tone of his voice was one that was used to getting his own way. The Zen master smiled and said: "We should discuss this matter over a cup of tea." When the tea was served, the master poured his visitor a cup. But when the cup was full, he didn't stop pouring. The tea began to spill over the table but the master kept on pouring. The professor watched the overflow until he could no longer restrain himself: "Enough! You are spilling the tea all over! Can't you see the cup is full?!" The master stopped pouring and said: "You are like this cup, so full of your own opinions and speculations that nothing more can be added. Come back to me when the cup is empty. Come back with an empty mind."

———-

"We don't see things as they are,

We see things the way we are."

—Anais Nin

Author Bio

John Arnold is a retired licensed clinical social worker who worked on the Oregon Coast as a mental health therapist, clinical supervisor, and consultant. He now lives with his wife in Visalia, California.

Appendix

With copyright © and attributions as printed, permission to reproduce is granted.

Understanding Therapy (Part 1)

Understanding Therapy (Part 2)

ANTs

Problem Solving Protocol (inter-/intra-agency)

Problem Solving Protocol (personal)

The Rules for Being Human

The Primary Parental Dilemma

Two Ideas to Encourage [Children's] Self-Esteem

Link to free printable handouts:

https://docs.google.com/document/d/1hdTyvElx6zxyDa1qFtBgm4d9162L_e1lUuxW3SwC2HU/edit?usp=sharing

Understanding Therapy (Part 1)

When we want to change things about ourselves that we don't like, most of us have an unrecognized thought that if we could just *understand why* things are the way they are, or how they got that way, we could be "fixed". Although we often don't realize it, many of us approach therapy to get answers to "why" questions. We assume the answers will give us the *understanding* that will change things. It turns out that understanding does help, but maybe only 50%, if that. The bottom line is that if you want change, then you actually have to change some things.

Behavior and emotional feelings (the stuff we want to change) have to do with things we believe and thoughts we have. Many of our beliefs developed early, when we couldn't reason so well. We made "sense" of things with the limited wisdom of the newborn and toddler and teen. The beliefs that underlie aspects of ourselves that we don't like have been a part of us for so long we don't even know we have these thoughts and beliefs.

Therapy has to do with changing some of these beliefs (even if we don't know *all* of them) and replacing them with different thoughts – thoughts we can have now, as adults. Or, due to situations in the past which involved significant fear and trauma, these would be new thoughts and beliefs we can have now that we're safe (or can make ourselves safe). Thoughts precede feelings. Changing these thoughts will help change your feelings. Once feelings change, behaviors can change more easily. Extra help may be needed for addictive behaviors.

This process of making the desired changes is helped if your body, including your brain, are functioning reasonably close to how they were designed to function. More mundanely, this means that exercise, sleep habits, and diet actually matter. This could also include meditation/

relaxation. All these factors have been shown by recent brain science research to have significant benefits for emotional well-being and can be as, or sometimes even more, effective than medication.

More provocatively, making the changes you desire could include corrective medicine for your brain, much the same as when we use corrective lenses for our eyes if they don't work like they were designed to. This point about correcting or optimizing brain function may be especially important if the changes one wants to make have to do with genetic and biochemical problems like AD/HD, or Schizophrenia, Bipolar Disorder, some developmental challenges, or other major mental illnesses and severe problems with depression and/or anxiety. Sometimes the tasks of therapy described here or in Part 2 can be so challenging that it is simply unrealistic in our current society to accomplish these tasks without correcting brain chemistry, at least initially, if not for the longer term. Contrary to popular but inaccurate opinion, if these medicines are prescribed by competent, knowledgeable, and experienced prescribers of behavioral medicine, these drugs actually help you be you rather than drugging you into somebody you are not. Regardless, when medicine is indicated, the efforts one makes in psychotherapy may then be more effective.

Understanding Therapy (Part 2)

The seeming audacity that is represented in producing two one-page handouts with these titles is not unrecognized by the writer. Aside from my tendency toward mischievous humor, as I've gotten older and even more simple, simplicity in understanding complex matters has become more important to me in my attempts to communicate more effectively with the brave people that take the risk of therapy. Since the process and experience of therapy is challenging and at times painful, it seems to me that the more we understand the process, the less likely we are as clients to try to escape the emotional challenges of doing therapy by means of cognitive (intellectual) defenses.

This second part of "Understanding Therapy" complements Part 1. In the name of simplicity, I'm suggesting that these two parts are all one needs to "know" about therapy. While knowing about the "bare bones" of therapy can be helpful, it in no way precludes the need for going through the process, or the experience, of the doing of therapy.

Part 2 of understanding therapy has to do with what I believe to be a remarkable and significant discrepancy in Western Culture between our cognitive understanding of how feelings are created and controlled and the experiential practice of dealing with our emotions in day-to-day life. What is so astounding about the discrepancy is that it is generally not talked about directly, even by many mental health professionals. I believe this lack of discussion doesn't have to do with conscious avoidance as much as it has to do with how pervasive and, therefore, insidious this culturally reinforced discrepancy is.

What exactly is the discrepancy? It can be described like this: Ask most reasonably thoughtful, knowledgeable people "Who is in control of and responsible for your feelings?" and the usual answer is "Well, I am, of course". However, if you follow that question up with "So why is it that on a mostly daily basis you blame other people and circumstances and even inanimate objects for how you feel?", the person you're asking will look a little confused and might eventually even start arguing with you or imagining that you are simply playing some kind of intellectual word game. In point of fact, the confusion is a result of this very discrepancy that goes largely unexamined by most of us. We believe one thing and regularly operate as if we believe something else, e.g., "That makes me mad.", "She really ticks me off.", "It is so irritating." What actually happens is that we make ourselves angry, we make ourselves feel. Unlike the song's refrain "You make me feel...." it would be much more accurate, though not poetic, if the refrain read "I make me feel like a natural woman." The idea that other people and things "make us feel" is as irrational as the psychotic symptom of "thought insertion" where the person struggling with a psychotic illness has a belief that some other person is responsible for their thoughts. In daily practice we live in a culture that has the arguably collective psychotic belief of "feelings insertion". When our prefrontal cortex has been compromised by emotions, like anger, we actually lose, temporarily, I.Q. points and it is especially easy then to believe that someone else created that emotion in us. In turn, it is then easy, at that moment, to believe stupid behaviors are O.K.

Of course this is not some new idea. I'm simply reporting through personal and professional experience that which the great thinkers, teachers, and spiritual leaders have talked about for centuries: the importance of "knowing thyself" and looking inward for the "answers" to Life's questions. Part 2 of understanding therapy is coming to accept that we are actually capable of creating, as well as not creating, our own feelings. At that point of understanding we are ready to deal with and do the actual work of therapy which is to practice the application of this understanding on a daily basis. The empowerment and healing that can take place because of the acceptance of this understanding can be remarkable.

ANTS

(Automatic Negative Thoughts)

Cognitive Behavioral Therapy (CBT)

A = Activating event (trigger)

B = Belief about the event (the "tape" or movie we have after we're triggered)

C = Emotional consequence (the emotional response we have to the belief)

D = Behavioral consequence (the actions we take as a result of the emotional response)

Four Questions:

1. Is the thought true?
2. Can I absolutely know that it's true?
3. How do I react when I believe that thought?
4. Who would I be without the thought? Or how would I feel if I didn't have the thought?

Credit: Daniel Amen, MD

Problem Solving Protocol -Inter/Intra-Agency

1. Communicate your perception of the problem to the person(s) *directly*

Some guidelines for doing this effectively:

► Stick to behaviors; things you can actually see ...or think you see. (Forget about your subjective judgments regarding the other's character or incompetence or your assumptions about their motivational intent *regardless* of how accurate and astute you think your perceptions are.)

► If you *must* assume, assume there's an *information gap* between you and the other. Also assume that the other is like you: a good person trying to do the best s/he can, with what s/he understands, in order to make things better. (Believe it or not, *this* assumption will be correct 999 times out of 1,000.)

► Express yourself in an *emotionally neutral* manner. (Emotionally laden expressions of concern indicate that the perceived problem has been prejudged by you. This encourages defensiveness which impedes listening; both of which cost time (& $), feel lousy, and interfere with our professional business.)

► In talking to another, try using the structure: "I thought I saw *x* ", "I thought *y*", "So I felt *z*", maybe followed by, "Thought I'd better see you for a perception check". End of statement. Don't talk too much.

If you use language in a manner that acknowledges the fallibility of your perception and that others' behavior is *not* in fact responsible for how you feel, the other is less likely to be organized to screen your information through defensiveness.

► Be open to the possibility that *you* may be misinformed or have misperceived or that *you* have something to learn (strange, but true). Be open to the possibility of *partial* truths and *partial* errors. After all, we're not required to operate inside the confines of the "absolute", Aristotelian, either/or, black/white, polarized reality that is framed by political rhetoric and the mass media.

***Remember*:** Our **professional** concerns are with **functions,** not your perceptions of the personal attributes of colleagues. Focus on functions, the *tasks* of our job. **When confused, seek clarification, not judgments.**

When this process is followed and the response you get is not satisfactory:

2. Communicate your perception of the dissatisfactory resolution *directly to the person(s)* and let him/her know that you think it would behoove the two (or more) of you to discuss this with your supervisor(s) at a joint meeting.

At this point (#2) the person(s) you're trying to communicate with *may* find additional motivational reserves to help find a mutually satisfactory solution or s/he may *also* desire a third party to help facilitate a solution. If the person(s) balks at the notion of a supervisor's involvement but you believe further discussion at this time would be unproductive, you are now on solid footing to say words to the effect "I'm sorry, but I'm *required* by policy to involve the supervisor at this point." (The supervisor(s), too, have good ground on which to get involved since both of you have talked about the problem directly. Of course, either party can involve an additional staff person to attend if such support is seen as helpful.)

Please remember, as challenging as this model might be to enact, it is a professionally appropriate process, it is a sound management practice, it is consistent with what we advise our clients and, most importantly, it is more likely to solve problems early (i.e., #1 above) and result in healthier, more professionally satisfying work relationships. Besides, the more you do it, the easier it is. Also, no matter what the outcome, you can feel good about *your* attempt, which is better than feeling angry, impotent, and frustrated.

Problem Solving Protocol-Personal

Communicate your perception of the problem to the person(s) *directly* (not to a 3rd party unless it's to consult or vent; you don't like it when someone communicates a concern about you via another person; so Guess What?: no one else likes it either)

Some guidelines for doing this effectively:

▶ Stick to behaviors; things you can actually see ...or think you see. (Forget about your subjective judgments regarding the others character or incompetence or your assumptions about their motivational intent *regardless* of how accurate and astute you think your perceptions are.)

▶ If you *must* assume, assume there's an *information gap* between you and the other. Also assume that the other is like you: a good person trying to do the best s/he can, with what s/he understands, in order to make things better. (Believe it or not, *this* assumption will be correct 999 times out of 1,000.)

▶ Express yourself in an *emotionally neutral* manner. (Emotionally laden expressions of concern indicate that the perceived problem has been prejudged by you. This encourages defensiveness which impedes listening; both of which cost time (& $), feel lousy, and interfere with the task at hand.)

▶ In talking to another, try using the structure: "I thought I saw *x*", "I thought *y*", "So I felt *z*", maybe followed by, "Thought I'd better see you for a perception check". End of statement. Don't talk too much. If you use language in a manner that acknowledges the fallibility of your perception where the behavior of others does *not*, in fact, create how you feel, the other is less likely to be organized to screen your information through defensiveness, i.e., talk about how *you* feel and not how the other "made you feel". (The psycho-neurological process of how feelings are actually created in humans is a different subject than the one being addressed here. Suffice it to say, the myth being perpetrated and reinforced on an unsuspecting society by the standard language conventions "you made me mad", "that frustrates me", "what he said made me angry" is no more true than the validity of blaming someone for something that happened in one of your dreams. The "mechanism of action" as to how feelings are actually created, and controlled, is a different topic of discussion.)

►Be open to the possibility that *you* may be misinformed or have misperceived or that *you* have something to learn (unlikely but possible). Be open to the possibility of *partial* truths and *partial* errors. (After all, we're not required to operate inside the confines of the "absolute", either/or, black/white, polarized reality that is framed by political rhetoric and mainstream mass media.)

Remember: The issues that actually concern you have to do with **functions**, i.e., with some*thing* not working right, not your perceptions of the personal attributes of the person(s). In other words, focus on the problem as the problem, not the person that you perceive the problem coming from.

When confused, seek clarification, not judgments.

Lastly, as challenging as this model might be to follow, it is more likely to solve problems and result in healthier relationships. It is also more likely to help you learn, without anger or bitterness, when certain relationships are not healthy for you and should be avoided. And the more you try to practice these ideas, the easier it becomes. Also, no matter what the outcome, you can feel good about *your* attempt to solve a problem, which is better than feeling angry, impotent, and frustrated.

The Rules for Being Human

1. You Will Receive A Body – You may like it or hate it, but it will be yours for the entire period.

2. You Will Learn Lessons – You are enrolled in a full-time informal school called Life. Each day in this school you have the opportunity to learn lessons. If you can actually recognize the opportunity, you may like the lessons or think them irrelevant and hence choose to ignore them, no matter, keep reading.

3. A Lesson Is Repeated Until Learned – A lesson will be presented to you in various forms until you have learned it. When you have learned it, you can then go on to the next lesson.

4. There Are No Mistakes, Only Lessons – Growth is a process of trial and error; experimentation. The "failed" experiments are as much a part of the process as the experiment that ultimately "works".

5. Learning Lessons Does Not End – There is no part of life that does not contain its lessons. If you are alive, there are lessons to be learned.

6. "There" Is No Better Than "Here" – When your "there" has become a "here" you will simply obtain another "there" that will, again, look better than "here".

7. Others Are Merely Mirrors Of You – You cannot love or hate something about another person unless it reflects to you something you love or hate about yourself.

8. Your Answers Lie Only Inside Of You – The answers to Life's questions lie only inside of you. All you need to do is look, listen, and trust.

9. You Will Forget All This

—Anonymous

The Primary Parental Dilemma

Children need skills to deal with the challenges of life, especially the skills to handle disappointment and loss. Although we don't want our children to experience these things, they will anyway because change is the nature of life and we humans have very little control of most changes that life sends our way.

Children gain these necessary skills through the process of their parents *not allowing* them to do what they want and *requiring* them to do what they don't want. Nonetheless, children are like adults in that they would *prefer* to do what they want to do when they want to do it. Unlike most of us parents, children don't know how to put off doing what they want, e.g., they are not born with the ability to work now, get paid later.

Confusingly, there is nothing "wrong" with children testing limits or looking for the "loopholes" in parental structure. In fact, it is their *job* to find wiggle room in the directives that parents give them. (Actually, if they didn't try to "manipulate" their world to their own desires, it would be an indicator that something is really amiss.) Fortunately, it is the job of parents to plug the loopholes.

However, as parents we know that if we do not love our children by defending and advocating for them, no one else will. We also know that if we do not love our children by holding them accountable for their choices and actions, they will grow up handicapped – much the same way that a butterfly's ability to fly is damaged or destroyed if some well-meaning human snips a few silk cocoon threads to "make it a little easier" for the butterfly to emerge. If a child is seen by the parents to have already had a rough start in life (e.g., due physical or developmental handicaps or due to child abuse or separation of birth parents, etc.), loving parents may try to "make it a little easier" by not being as firm as they might otherwise be. This tendency is even more powerful if parents feel "guilty" for lousy things that occurred earlier to their children.

Since we know that effective parenting includes the love of giving and protecting as well as the love of setting boundaries and saying "no", the primary dilemma for us parents is having the wisdom of when to do which.

For some reason, certain boundaries are easier to set than others. We seem to have less trouble requiring our children to get dressed before they go outside, to eat most foods with utensils, to not play in the street, and to bathe somewhat regularly. Generally speaking, the boundaries we most care about have to do with values and safety. *How* we go about solving the primary parental dilemma when it arises (and it does so constantly) is beyond the scope of this brief note. There are many resources that can aid parents in dealing with this dilemma but the point here is that a) you are not alone; you share this particular challenge with all parents and b) this dilemma needs to be resolved effectively, at a minimally adequate level, most of the time so that our children will have the tools they need to deal with life when we are not around to help.

Remember: There are no "good" parents. Our goal is to be "good enough" parents. Also remember, that when we do our best to set thoughtful, developmentally appropriate limits, our children will not hate or disown us... no matter what they might say to us at the moment that they discover that they are not going to get their way.

Two Ideas to Encourage Self-Esteem

1. *Just Don't Say No* Although a commonly accepted idea, praising positive behaviors, as well as acknowledging the absence of negative ones, tends to be difficult for us parents in daily practice. Our society tends to be unwittingly pathology-based. In the adult-to-child mindset of guidance and correcting behaviors, it seems to be easier for us to see what's "wrong", or to try to assign blame, than it is to see what's "right". On average, children hear exasperated statements like "No", "Stop that", and "I thought I told you...." much more often than praise and positive acknowledgement.

Negative feedback, especially a lot of it, has the unfortunate side effect of diminishing self-esteem. So, even though it may not sound profound, look for what's positive, be aware of the absence of the negative, and praise accordingly. In doing so, you may even see more positives than you knew existed. You will also be reinforcing positive behavior which turns out to be developmentally healthier and more effective than trying to extinguish negative behavior with negatives. It feels better, too.

2. *Validation* Feeling and believing that you're *understood* by others is more important to us humans than having others be in *agreement* with us. When it comes to the children we care about, we grown-ups have a tendency to want to remove or "talk them out of" bad feelings or worries they may have. We also have a tendency to defend ourselves from their angry, verbal attacks so as to "set them straight". Unfortunately, when we do either of these we run the risk of leaving our children feeling that we don't understand them. Whether or not our children are "right" or "wrong", accurate or inaccurate about the issue at hand, they do not have the experience or developmental resources that we do to weather situations of feeling misunderstood by the adults who are significant to them. Thus, they are even more likely than grown-ups to personalize the perception of being misunderstood. This, in turn, facilitates self-doubt and a lowering of self-esteem.

When a child expresses sadness or worry, for instance, try simply acknowledging (reflecting back) that they must feel pretty lousy. If you don't try to argue them out of their feelings by using adult knowledge or logic, the understanding you've conveyed will be more likely to free them up to talk more about the perceived worry or sad situation. (*Talking out* feelings is helpful; *acting out* feelings can be a problem.) If they feel that they're talking to someone who understands, they are more likely to listen to your advice – especially when your advice happens later in the conversation and comes in the way of a suggestion or something that works for you when you've had the same feeling.

When a child expresses anger, especially if directed at you, acknowledge (with caring and genuineness) that you know they are angry and you're sorry that they have to feel that right now. Maybe let them know that you might feel the same way if you were them and that one of the tough things about being a kid is having to be told what to do by grown-ups, or having to deal with things that don't seem fair. Being understanding does not have to diminish being firm, and being firm does not have to be "packaged" in a manner that children see as being "mean".

Even when children don't "get their way" in matters that would be unhealthy for their development, they can still feel understood (whether or not they acknowledge that to you at the time.) If they feel understood, they feel connected. The feeling of "connectedness" fosters self-esteem.

End Notes

[1] "Strength-based" is a professional jargon phrase that unfortunately is often used as meaning a perfunctory list of client strengths such as "good hygiene", "adequate commitment to therapy", "superior intelligence", etc., and as might be required on some agency assessment form. It is referred to here as viewing clients and using non-pathology-based language that infers one's clients are like yourself: a good person doing the best they can when dealing with the challenges of life.

[2] Having a spouse see the same therapist that their spouse is seeing for individual therapy is not a common or necessarily advisable practice due to ethical considerations regarding dual relationships and "boundary crossings". When I asked Gert what she thought about seeing my wife, she waved her hand in dismissal and said "I take everyone as they come" by which she meant that she could ethically compartmentalize and be exclusively with whatever client was then in her presence. There are exceptions to every rule. Gert was one of those. She was exceptional.

[3] There are many scholarly articles on the subject of language, emotions, emotional control, and neuroscience. For example, see "Language and Emotion: Introduction to the Special Issue" of *The Journal of Affective Science* by Kristen A Lindquist. However, apart from not specifically addressing the discrepancy premise of this book, these research-based, academic writings are not well-known and the readability renders them highly inaccessible to the general public. I am not a scholar. But I mention the reference to additional scientific literature in an attempt to lend credence to the fact that the premise of this book was not fabricated out of whole cloth.

[4] One of the concepts of General Systems Theory (See Ludwig von Bertalanffy, 1946) is that of "homeostatic equilibrium". Complex systems, like the brain, or a human family, like to stay the same. To change the system, a part of the system has to change so that the general system can find a new equilibrium or balance.

[5] It should be noted that not all presenting problems for which a child or adolescent might be referred for therapy result in working with the "identified patient" via the modality of individual therapy. The reasons why a child or adolescent is referred for psychotherapy can have many different etiologic causes, including more than one. Trauma is only one possibility. Problems can be nested in family dynamics, inadequate child management, biochemical and/or developmental problems, etc. Referral, made by parent(s) or legal guardian, is usually made for individual therapy. "That kid needs counseling!" The mode of therapy should be based on competent evaluation which, in turn, determines which mode of treatment might be most effective. A few times when a child was referred to me, I never saw the referred child. After initial assessment with parents, I sometimes found myself continuing to work with the parents alone.

www.ingramcontent.com/pod-product-compliance
Lightning Source LLC
LaVergne TN
LVHW051058210926
848486LV00025B/423/J
* 9 7 9 8 3 4 9 4 7 7 5 2 2 *